GLOBAL CREATIVE ARCHITECTURE

AUTHOR M.A. DIPL. ING. DANIEL SCHULZ

SELECTED WORKS OF WORLD ARCHITECTS

LINKS

Published in 2008 by:
Page One Publishing Private Limited
20 Kaki Bukit View
Kaki Bukit Techpark II
Singapore 415956
Tel: (65) 6742-2088
Fax: (65) 6744-2088
enquiries@pageonegroup.com
www.pageonegroup.com

First published 2008 by Liaoning Science and Technology Press

Project Manager: Daniel Schulz
Project Manager: Dawn Teo
Cover design: Beverly Chong

All rights reserved. No part of this publication may be reproduced, stored in any retrieval system or transmitted, in any form or by any means, electronic, mechanical, photocopying, recording or otherwise, without prior permission in writing from the publisher. For information, contact Page One Publishing Private Limited, 20 Kaki Bukit View, Kaki Bukit Techpark II, Singapore 415956.

Printed by SNP Leefung Printers (Shenzhen) Co. Ltd.

GLOBAL CREATIVE ARCHITECTURE
Copyright © 2008 Page One

First published in 2007 by:
Links International
Jonqueres, 10, 1-5
08003 Barcelona, Spain
Tel: (34) 93 301 21 99
Fax: (34) 93 301 00 21
E-mail: info@linksbooks.net
www.linksbooks.net

Distributed by:
Links International
Jonqueres, 10, 1-5
08003 Barcelona, Spain
Tel: +34 93 301 21 99
Fax: +34 93 301 00 21

ISBN 978-84-96263-91-8

CONTENTS
GLOBAL CREATIVE ARCHITECTURE

OFFICE

- 006 SCHWENNINGER BKK
- 012 ZUBLIN HEADQUARTER Z-ZWO
- 018 COMPETENCE CENTER INNSBRUCK
- 024 RWE TOWER
- 030 HYPOVEREINSBANK LUXEMBOURG
- 036 MAX-PLANCK-INSTITUT FFM
- 042 A3 EDINBURGH PARK
- 048 OFFICE LAVAAL
- 054 RIJKSWATERSTAAT ZEELAND
- 060 GALLILEO
- 066 CARTIER HEAD OFFICE
- 072 KSR

INDUSTRIAL

- 078 KRYSTAL
- 084 SEMPERIT
- 090 RE-TEM FACTORY
- 096 VIT-INDUSTRIAL BUILDING ASPERHOFEN
- 102 OTTEN FACTORY & OFFICE BUILDING
- 108 PRINTING HOUSE CARINTHIA
- 114 NESPRESSO
- 120 ALPLA

PUBLIC

- 126 STADTHAUS
- 132 JR SAITAMA STATION
- 138 FESTHALLE WEISSACH
- 144 BUBBLETECTURE M
- 150 SURUGA KINDERGARTEN

HOUSING

- 156 EDDI'S HOUSE
- 162 C+R GRABHER HOUSE
- 168 RESIDENCE KLOSTERNEUBURG
- 174 HOUSE IN BISHAMON
- 180 SINGLE FAMILY HOUSE IN GAUTING
- 186 FISCHER-STEGEN RESIDENCE

RESIDENTIAL

- 192 SEEWUERFEL
- 198 MONTEVIDEO
- 204 KENYUEN
- 210 SPITTELAU VIADUCTS HOUSING
- 216 RIVER HEIGHTS
- 222 HOHENBÜHL
- 228 LIVING AT THE SUN
- 234 COLONIE

MUSEUM

- 240 MERCEDES-BENZ
- 246 ORDRUPGAARD MUSEUM EXTENSION
- 252 BMW SHOWROOM
- 258 TOUR DE MORON

- 262 INDEX

ABOUT THE AUTHOR

M.A. Dipl. Ing. Daniel Schulz
Diploma Engineer at Wismar University / Germany
Master of Arts in Architecture at Wismar University / Germany
Master of Architecture at Shenyang Architecture University / China

2001 IS Schwerin – Engineering and Architecture Company
2002 Ivan Rijavec Architects - Melbourne / Australia
2004 New World Architects – Beijing / China
2005 IGEL – Institute for Design - Energy & Light Planning – Wismar / Germany
2006 Shenyang Architecture and Urban Planning Institute – Shenyang / China

GLOBAL CREATIVE ARCHITECTURE
PREFACE

Global Creative Architecture shows the newest and most important work of architects worldwide.

Architecture today is characterized by manifold styles and forms but with the aim of finding new sustainable solutions for our living environment. Function and shape, technology, sustainability and economic viability — all these criteria designed in the building demand creativity from the architect. The collection of Global Creative Architecture aims to give the public access to the current state of modern, creative architecture. Invited architects from Germany, Austria, Netherlands, Switzerland, Belgium, Japan, England and Australia are collected in this book.

More and more creative architecture is needed in the architectural market in the future. This book aims to show high quality and creative architecture to the public based on deep conceptual aspects such as analogies to the respective place, function, shapes and material. Readers will find great inspiration in the collected works.

OFFICE
SCHWENNINGER BKK
WULF & PARTNER

Client:	Schwenninger BKK K.d.ö.R.
Construction costs:	approx. € 16.5 mill
Work started:	11 / 2002
Completion:	8 / 2005

A new four-storey office building with a central hall for various purposes (cafeteria, conferences etc.) and an open atrium, three upper floors for office use and an underground car park. The facade is fronted with floor-to-ceiling vertical adjustable sunshading elements. Innovative energy concepts include geothermal sources using thermally activated bored piles.

With the design of the new central administration of the "Schwenninger BKK", a dynamic prospering health insurance, the goal was pursued to create a conceptual and innovative administration building which portrays the business through its architecture. Functional and basic content-related elements were also consistently transferred as elements of art and design, or climate and building technology.

The building represents itself as a markedly urban element and at the same time, as a differentiated architectural prelude to the city. The architecture is also shaped in the ground plan by its clear structure of the building. A central four-storey entrance hall which passes over into an open atrium. The east side of the atrium opens towards the lake.

Tobias Wulf   Kai Bierich   Alexander Vohl

south elevation | photo Brigida Gonzalez

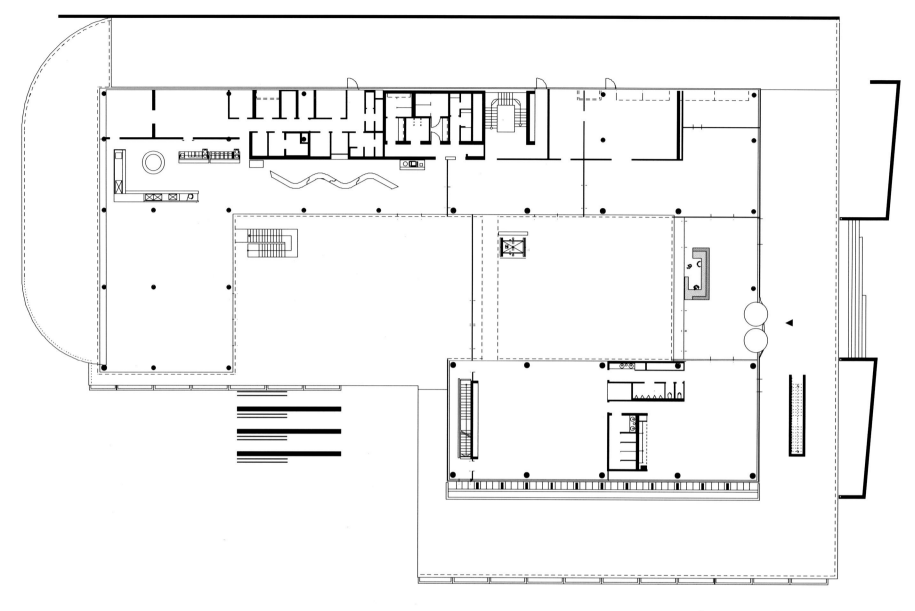

| ground plan | plan Wulf &. Partner |

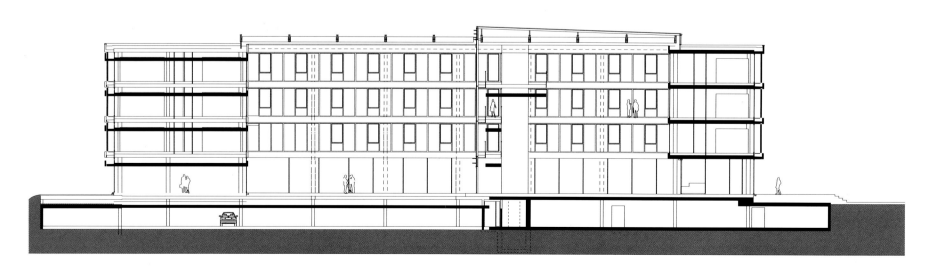

| section | plan Wulf &. Partner |

| south facade | photo Brigida Gonzalez |

| office view | photo Brigida Gonzalez |
| sun shade facade | photo Brigida Gonzalez |

| courtyard | photo Brigida Gonzalez

OFFICE
ZUBLIN HEADQUARTER Z-ZWO
EIKE BECKER_ARCHITECTS

Architect:	Eike Becker_Architects
Client:	Züblin Project Development
Function:	corporate headquarters
Team:	Eike Becker, Helge Schmidt, Julia Brunow, Boris Hassenstein, Irmgard Hermes, Christian Koch, Oliver Mehl, Beatriz Neske, Markus Pfeifer, Oliver Rednitz, Nina Schrick, David Steiner, Marc Winkler
Completion:	2002

Eike Becker   Helge Schmidt

Fifteen years after completion of their first headquarters in Stuttgart, the Züblin AG built another innovative headquarter building in the borough of Möhringen. Eike Becker_Architects won the competition in September 2000 and immediately started work on the final plans of this administration building for 350 staff members. The main design objectives were e-housing, new working environments and low-energy service technology.

south-east view | photo Roland Halbe

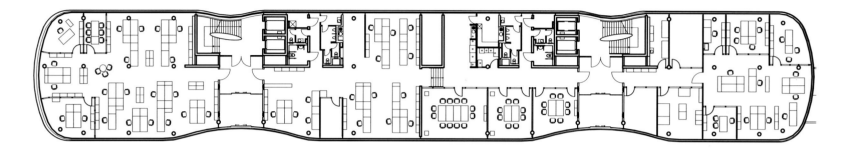

| ground plan | plan Eike Becker _ Architects |

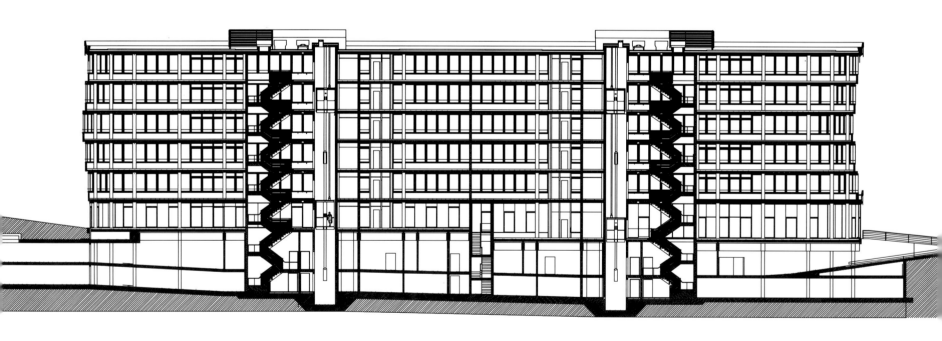

| section B-B | plan Eike Becker _ Architects |

| east elevation | photo Roland Halbe | 015

| south facade entrance | photo Roland Halbe |

| staircase | photo Roland Halbe |

| south facade | photo Roland Halbe |

OFFICE
COMPETENCE CENTER INNSBRUCK
AICHER ARCHITECTS

Gerhard Aicher

Project name: Competence Center Innsbruck
Completion: 2003
Architect: Aicher Architekten
Construction: Steel-concrete frame construction
Facade post-bolt construction
Use area: 3654 m²
Volume: 25 533 m³

The Competence Center Innsbruck was defined by the builder as an impulse center and technology center with national effect and part of an Austrian location network. The architecture and functionality was of high importance because of the contents of the center and its location in a strongly developed trade and business district. The building functions as a platform within this district through different infrastructures (foyer hall; seminar room; gastronomy; internet involvement, etc.). Because of the great interest in the rentable space of the house, the expansion of the Competence Center is already well underway.

| north-east view | photo Marc Lins

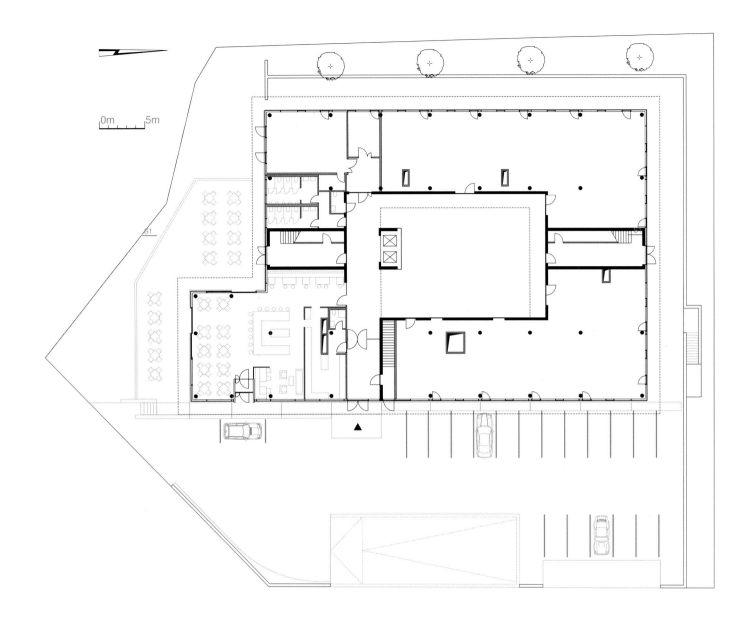

| ground plan | plan Aicher Architects |

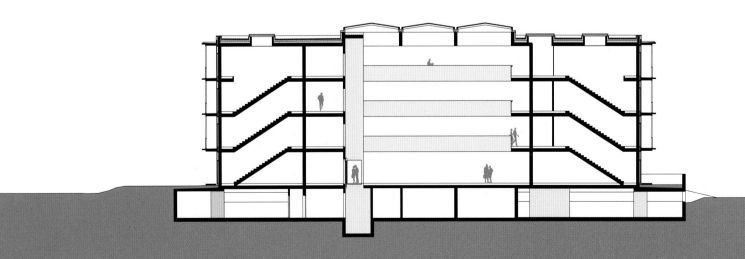

| selection A-A | plan Aicher Architects |

| east facade with entrance | photo Barbara Bühler

| east facade | photo Barbara Bühler |
| north facade | photo Barbara Bühler |

OFFICE
RWE TOWER
GERBER ARCHITEKTEN

Prof. Eckhard Gerber

Client:	DIAG GmbH & Co. KG II
Completion:	2005
Height:	99.9 m
GFA:	27 300 m²
Gross volume:	87 500 m³

The 22-storey-high tower with its lenticular floor plan consolidates the urban structure between the main station and the city centre, which had been dissatisfying to date. The curved facade of the 100-meter-high office building is clad in dark polished granite and is subdivided by single windows. Two mono pitch roofs sloping inwards form the upper end. The higher and more inclined section has been developed as a glass roof.

north-west elevation | photo Hans Jürgen Landes

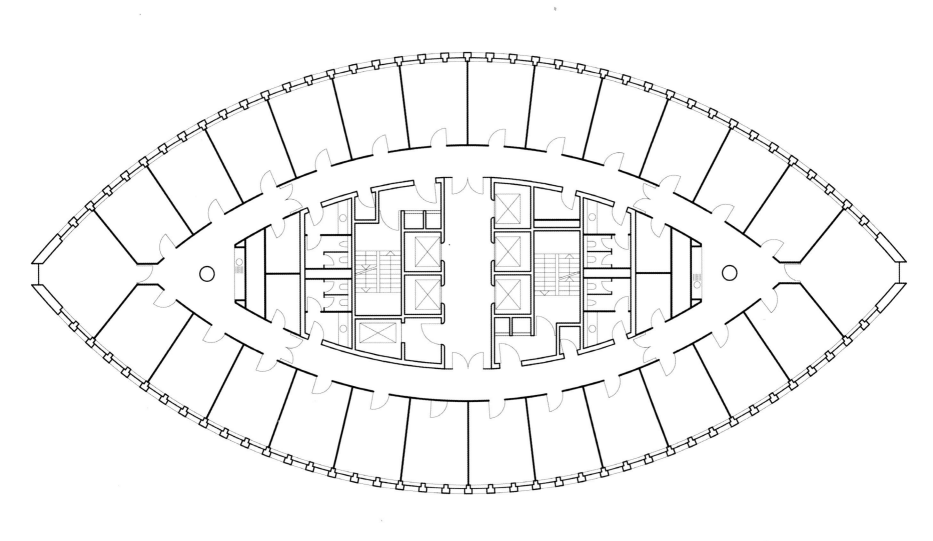

| ground plan regular floor | plan Gerber Architekten |

| south elevation | photo Hans Jürgen Landes | 027

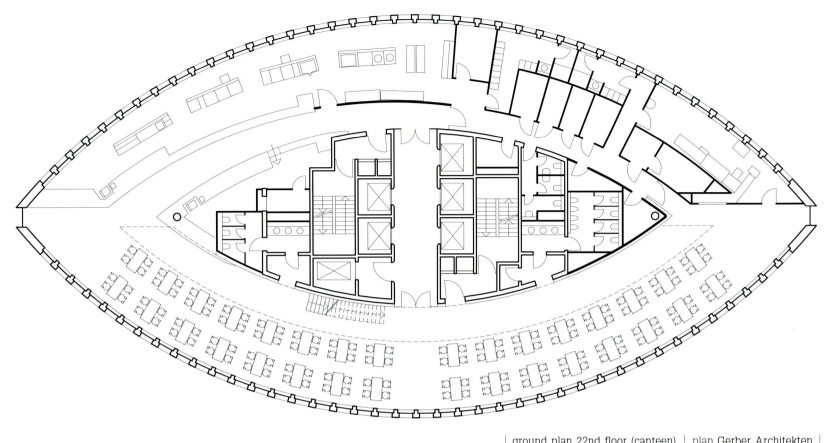

| ground plan 22nd floor (canteen) | plan Gerber Architekten |
| base of building | photo Hans Jürgen Landes |

OFFICE
HYPOVEREINSBANK LUXEMBOURG
ATELIER 5

Architect: Atelier 5
Completion: 2003
Client: HypoVereinsbank Luxembourg

The HypoVereinsbank is to be erected in a quarter that is almost completely reserved for bank buildings. According to an earlier development plan, solitary structures were placed in a row along the street. In contrast, the new edifice from Atelier 5 follows a new, modern urban concept by abutting the street over the course of 120 meters and achieves – in clear contrast to the individual, freestanding buildings – a spatial effect.

In addition, the bank makes its two main functions readable by means of two fully distinct building volumes. A compact head building, very open towards the outside, with reception hall, conference rooms and a restaurant, is connected to a narrow, long volume that appears more closed. The workspaces are to be found here.

While the head building has a relatively small volume and containing large space at times as well as a correspondingly large glazing area that requires air-conditioning, the administrative tract is ventilated via the windows and occupies only half of the exterior surface area – which fully suffices for the lighting because of the minimal building depth – and louvered sun-shading provides effective protection against heat gain. The rest of the facade is composed of stuccoed concrete together with the colonnades and the ceiling of the same material, which offer large thermal storage mass. A very ecological building has been created, with simple elements that are anything but banal!

Team Atelier 5

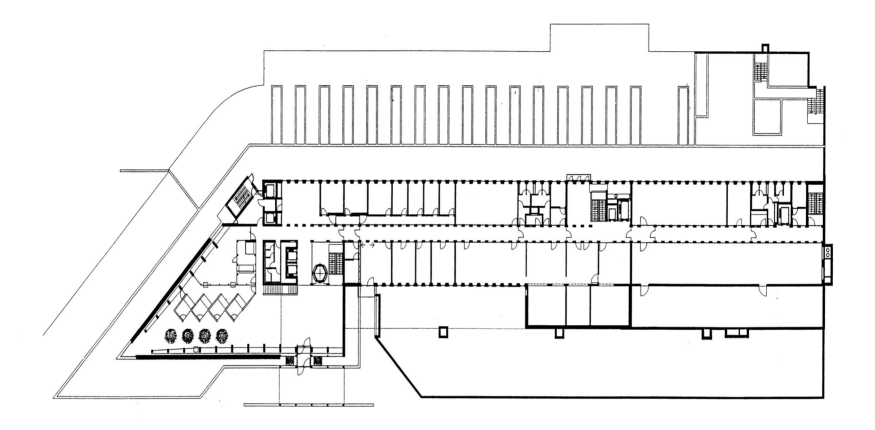

| ground plan ground floor | plan Atelier 5 |

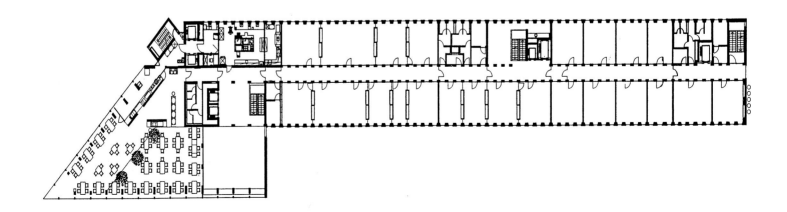

| ground plan 3rd floor | plan Atelier 5 |

north facade | photo Christian Richters

| south elevation | photo Christian Richters |
| floor view | photo Christian Richters |

OFFICE
MAX-PLANCK-INSTITUT FFM
AUER + WEBER + ARCHITEKTEN

Client: Max-Planck-Gesellschaft zur Förderung der Wissenschaften e.V.
Completion: 2003
Value: 33,2 M.€
GFA: 16 000 m²
Use: Office, Research, Laboratories

Prof. Fritz Auer   Prof. Carlo Weber

The three basic elements of the building are shaped differently according to their contents. The laboratory areas are located in the cubical building bodies on the north side, the areas for theoretical work are created by dispersed room groups which are oriented over "decks" to the south. In between is a hall, which connects both functional areas and serves as an orientation space and communication channel for the desirable exchange of ideas between theoretical and laboratory work.

The generous entrance area creates a north-south-connection between the chemistry and biology departments and serves as flexible space in the middle of the campus.

The hall space is defind on one hand through the monolithic concrete walls of the laboratory cube, and on the other hand through the rhythmic sequence of glass and wood wall elements at the opposite office areas.

Steel stairs, supplemented by bridges between the offices and laboratory, connect the building parts vertically and horizontally. A fine roof screen out of steel and glass spans the hall and casts different patterns of shadows on the walls and floor depending on the time of the day.

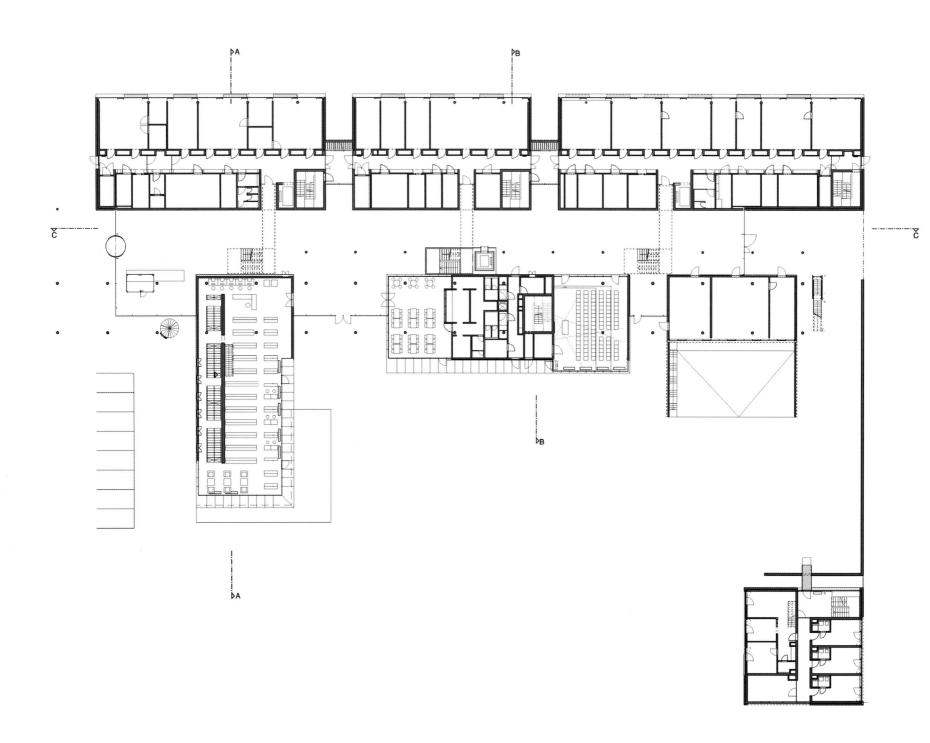

| ground plan | Plan Auer + Weber + Architekten |

library and landscape | photo Roland Halbe

| west elevation | photo Roland Halbe |
| main entrance and reception | photo Roland Halbe |

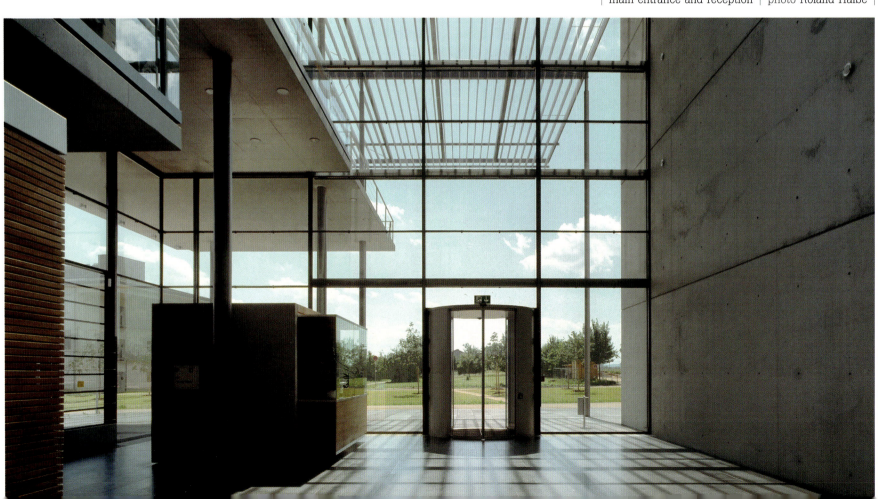

courdyard hall | photo Roland Halbe

OFFICE
A3 EDINBURGH PARK
GORDON MURRAY + ALAN DUNLOP

Alan Dunlop   Gordan Murray

Client:	New Edinburgh Limited
Site Start:	5 / 2000
Completion:	6 / 2001
Procurement:	Novated Design and Build
Value:	£7.5 million
Role:	Architects from Inception to Completion

Building A3, situated in Edinburgh Park and commissioned by New Edinburgh Limited, is the joint venture inspiration behind the park itself. It stands at the center of a group and encloses the main public space linking the piazza with the remainder of the park.

Associated with any plaza is the campanile, and in this building it has been used as a multi-functional device to signal the entrance to the building; to create an interesting public space between the building itself and its neighbour; and as a service-circulation core distinct from the building itself. The glass walls of the entrance link reinforce its freestanding nature.

The crystalline fragment of "rock" clad in a split face slate stands as a counter-point to the smooth cubist block that houses the financial centre itself, and in contrast to the slick classically laid out buildings of the terrace.

Internally, the building is divided longitudinally into open-plan space for group work-stations and cellular space. This creates a transparency through the building and clarity of organisation.

This building won the 2002 GIA Award.

south elevation | photo Andrew Lee | 043

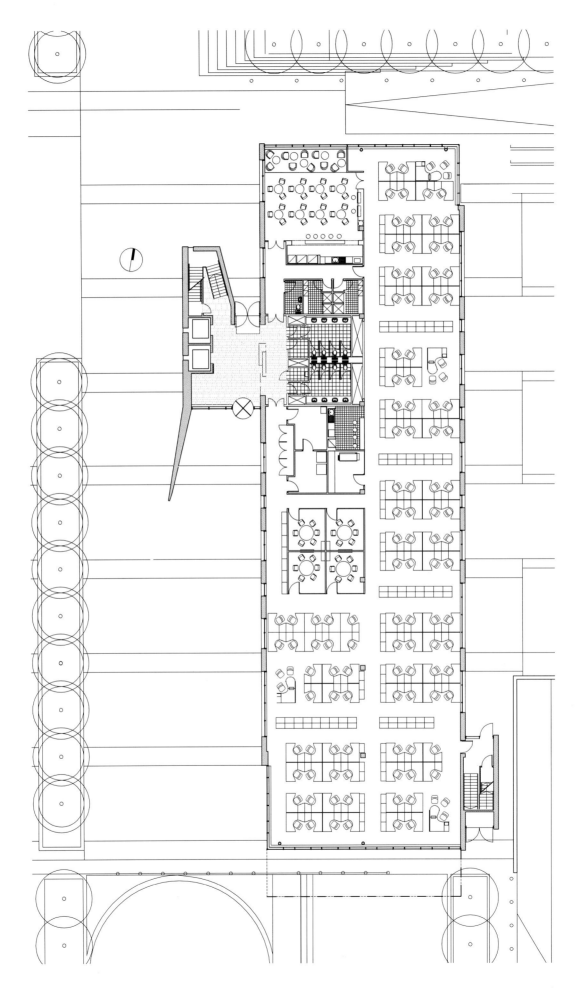

| entrance north elevation | photo Andrew Lee |

| foyer | photo Paul Zanre |

| west elevation | photo Paul Zanre |

OFFICE
OFFICE LAVAAL
GIOVANNI VACCARINI

Giovanni Vaccarini

Client: Lavaal srl
Completion: 11 / 2004
Site area: 8500 m² with park
Net effective area: 5000 m²

The new Lavaal's building offers spaces with multiple functions and organizational flexibility, with a system of mobile partitions based on an equipped floating pavement.

The concept is to create a building that houses the various functions and at the same time defines the public image of Lavaal.

The facade system comprises of two materials: the structural glass (creating transparency in all the spaces which comprise the work space), and the aluminum brise soleil.

The system of the brise soleil is interesting for at least two reasons: From the point of view of composition, it succeeds as a mobile facade. From the point of view of performance, it guarantees control of the light and the exposure to the sun.

south-east view | photo Alessandro Ciampi

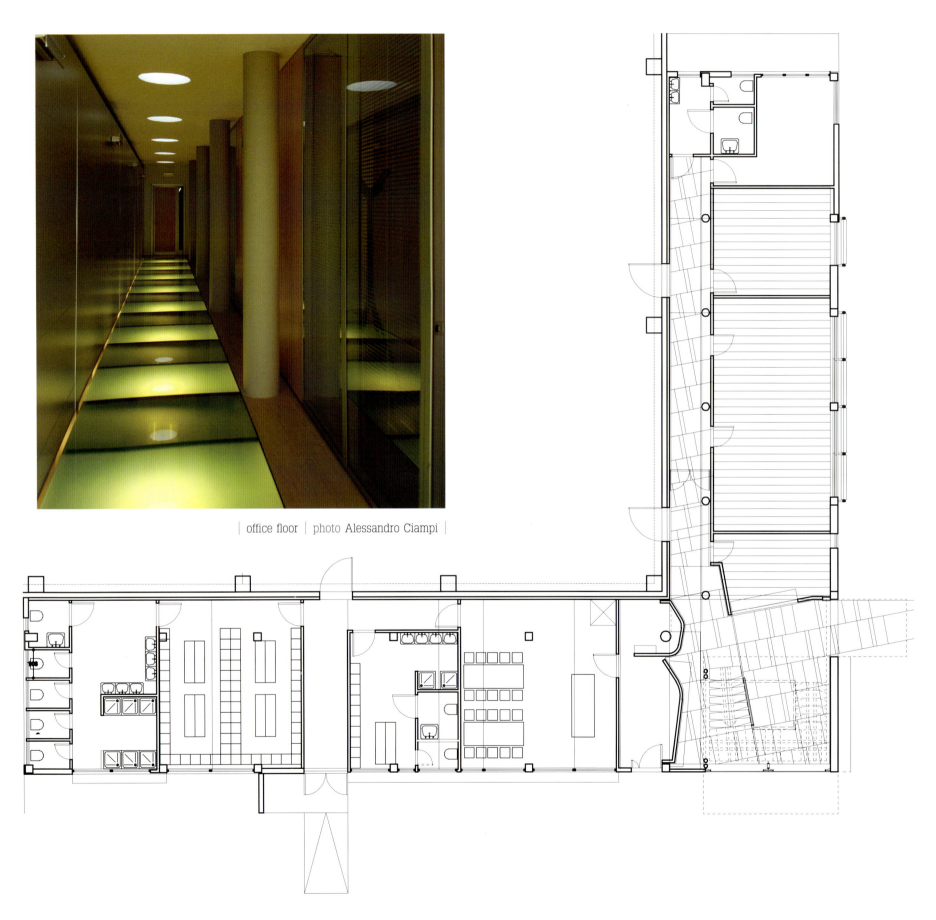

| office floor | photo Alessandro Ciampi |

| ground plan | plan Giovanni Vaccarini |

| lobby | photo Alessandro Ciampi

| entrance | photo Alessandro Ciampi |

| east facade | photo Alessandro Ciampi | 053

OFFICE
RIJKSWATERSTAAT ZEELAND
ARCHITECTENBUREAU PAUL DE RUITER BV

Client:	Government Building Agency, The Hague, the Netherlands
Completion:	11 / 2004
Site area:	12 761 m² with park
Net effective area:	2253 m²

The office for the Department of Water Management and Transport (RWS) fits into one long stretched transparent volume. By lifting the volume up, cars can be parked underneath the building. It has room for 450 workers, a 100%-guaranteed computer center which, in case of an emergency, can manage all the sluice-gates in the province of Zeeland (including the Delta works), a crisis centre, state archives, a restaurant, conference centre and a fitness centre. The flexible construction of the building and its installations make many divisions of the interior possible, from traditional to innovative office concepts. The office is a meeting point for its mostly outdoor working personnel and it stimulates the communication between them.

By using existing techniques in an innovative, smarter way, the building uses 50% less energy than other buildings. It saves and reuses energy by making use of passive solar energy, climate facades, atria, storage of cold and heat in the soil and active concrete.

Photo Koen van Domburg   Paul de Ruiter

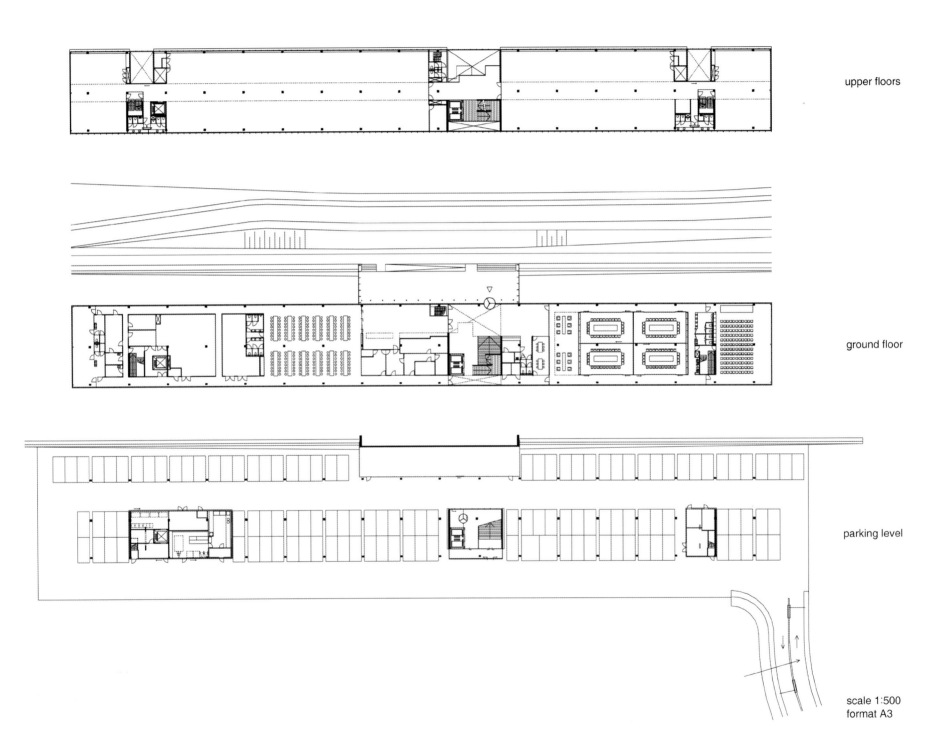

ground plan | plan Paul de Ruiter

south-west view | photo Pieter Kers / www.beeld.nu

OFFICE
GALLILEO
ARCHITEKTENGRUPPE N+M

Helmut Niehoff

Ulf Bambach

Client:	Dresdner Bank AG
Completion:	2003
Value:	190 M.€
GFA:	41 000 m²
Use:	Office

The high-rise consists of two components which are connected by a core, and was developed out of the urban situation (differentiation, height limitation, graded in heights to the Main and reception of the main directions of the surrounding streets). The low building follows the straight line of the "Kaiserstrasse" while the higher tower respects the "Gallus" structure.

Light, air and lightness were main criteria of the design. It was a main goal for the high-rise in spite of its limited height to work out a good proportion and/or a vertical proportion.

The opening of the core area in the centre creates attractive views east and west of the waiting areas of the elevators, at the same time creating transparency in the structure.

Ecological building standards include energy consevation concepts that enable an extremely economic and non-polluting operation of the building all year round.

south-east view | photo Joe Chambers

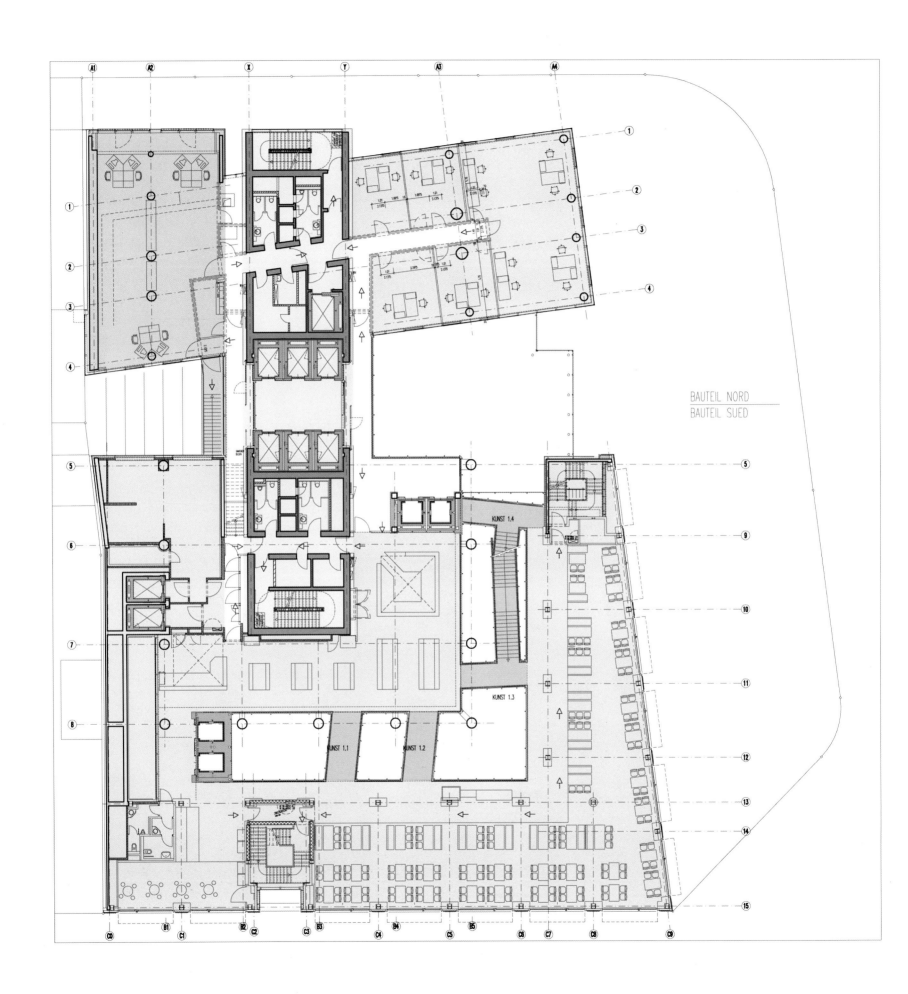

ground plan-first floor | plan Architektengroup N+M

south elevation | photo Wolfgang Toepfer

| tower | photo N+M |
| office view | photo N+M |

lobby view | photo Michael Kretzer

OFFICE
CARTIER HEAD OFFICE
RICARDO BOFILL TALLER DE ARQUITECTURA

Client:	Unibail
Surface area:	26 000 m²
Completion:	2003
Location:	Paris, France
Programme:	offices, shops, showroom, restaurant and bar, a multi-purpose hall, a gymnasium and parking space for 450 vehicles in the basement.

Ricardo Bofill

A complex of buildings in the heart of the 'Golden Triangle' (the 75008 arrondissement of Paris), close to the church of La Madeleine and Place de la Concorde. The project was conceived as a spatial and technical innovation whose source of inspiration is the city's covered streets and promenades. The exteriors of the buildings are combined in such a way that observers' perception of space changes each time, creating an interior block street with three access points and their corresponding addresses: 30, Rue du Faubourg Saint-Honoré; 33-37, Rue Boissy d'Anglas; and 3, Rue de Surène. The facades are of clear glass and serigraphed glass, while the paving is of pietra serena.

facade view | photo Fabrice Rambert & Arik Levy

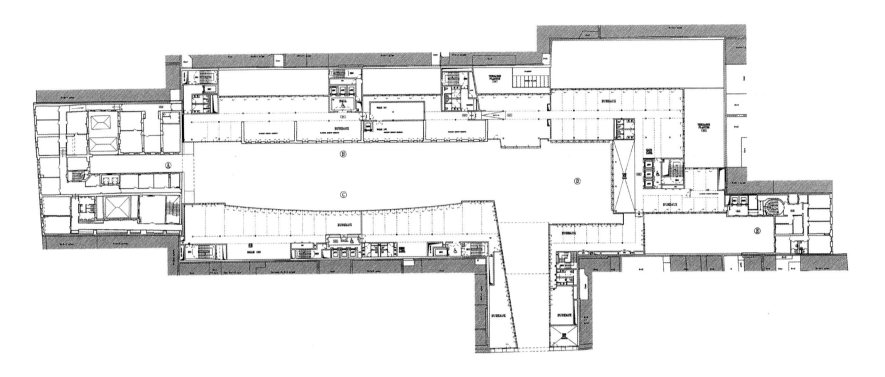

| ground floor plan | plan Ricardo Bofill |

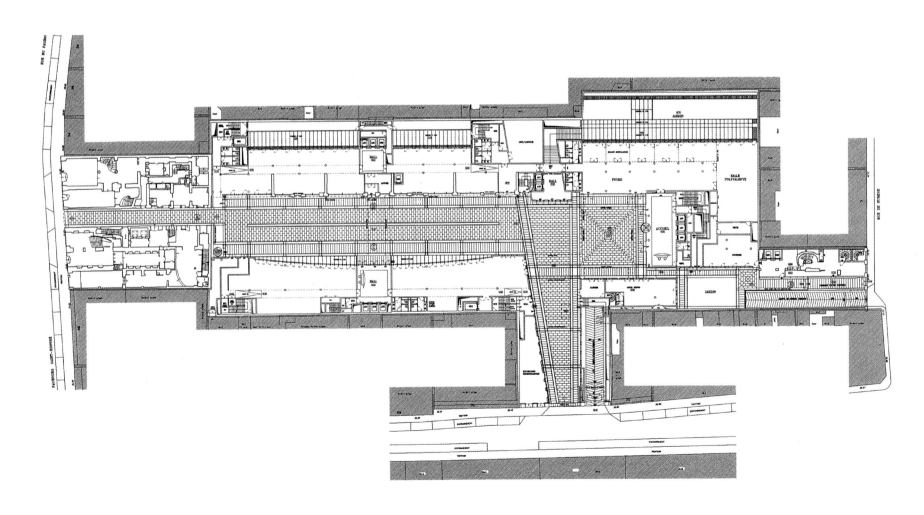

| first floor plan | plan Ricardo Bofill |

facade view | photo Fabrice Rambert & Arik Levy

| facade detail | photo Fabrice Rambert & Arik Levy |

| entrance | photo Fabrice Rambert & Arik Levy

OFFICE
KSR
HILMER & SATTLER U. ALBRECHT

Hilmer   Albrecht   Sattler

Completion: 2003
Use: Office

The expansion of the Karl-Scharnagl-Ring in front of the Bavarian State Chancellery is given a southern boundary by this eight-story tower. A second office building borders the street space that continues the ring road around the old part of the city in a southern direction. The ensemble can thereby be understood as making a contribution to the theme of "urban architecture".

All four sides of the building will have terraced surfaces of varying depths. The building's succinctness is heightened by its northern two-storeyed entrance that leads into the covered inner courtyard of eight storeys. This courtyard allows everyone who makes use of the building to participate in the spatial impression that it makes.

The other six-storey building, of about 100 meters in height, is staggered over five storeys according to the existing structural conditions in the adjoining side street. Two separate entrances give the building the necessary flexibility.

Both of the buildings are clad in terracotta facing, as is the case with the Maximilaneum, the Bayerische Landtag (Bavarian state parliament), that still has an effect on the bordering Maximilian Street. Despite their high proportion of glass, both buildings exhibit architectonic mass and are in conscious contrast to the neighbouring glass and metal cladded architecture. The supports of the lower building are unusual in the asymmetry of their profiles. In the tower building soft, rounded corners dominate, while the flatter building has profiles with sharp angles. The two buildings exhibit refined structural differences.

Double-glazed windows with metal casement on the outside and wooden casement on the inside ensure noise and emissivity reduction. A translucent sun screen lies in the space between the two layers.

south facade | photo Stefan Müller

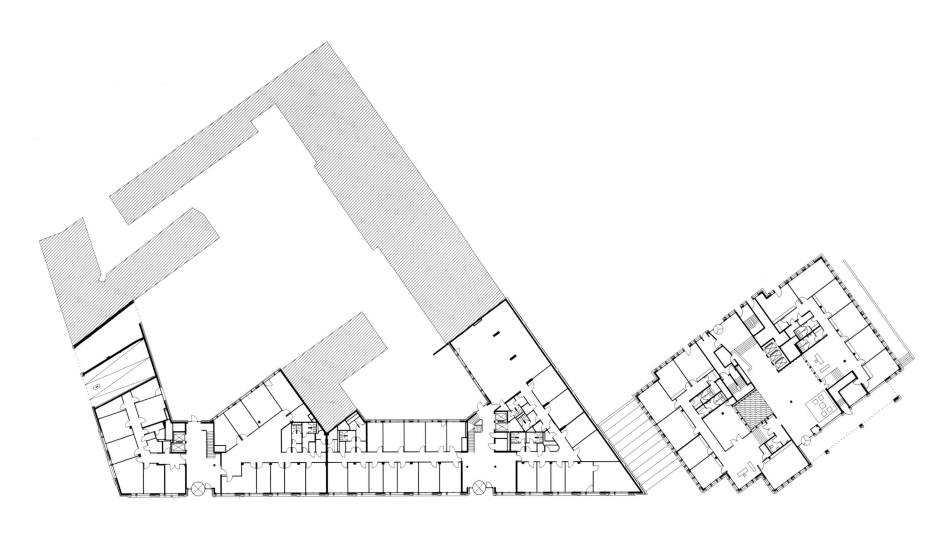

| ground plan | plan Hilmer & Sattler u. Albrecht |

south-west view | photo Stefan Müller

| facade | photo Stefan Müller |

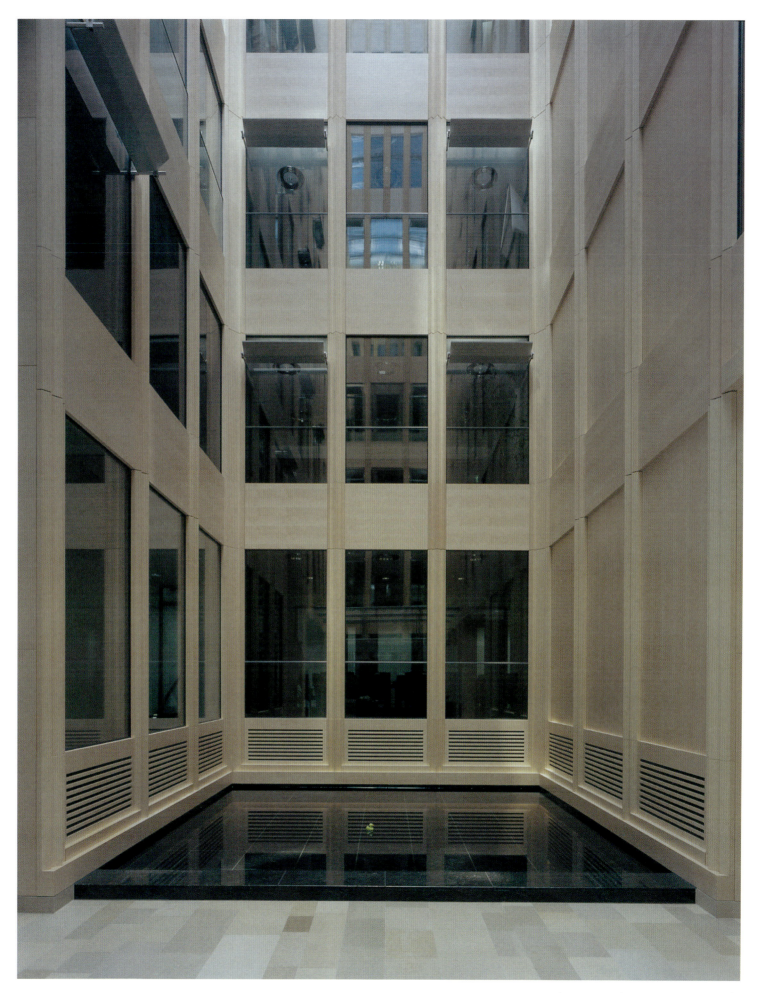

INDUSTRIAL
KRYSTAL
WULF & PARTNER

Tobias Wulf — Kai Bierich — Alexander Vohl

Client:	krystaltech Immobilien GmbH
Completion:	2003
Value:	11 M.€
Use:	office

Dynamics, flexibility and communication sum up the concept of the new European Headquarters of Krystaltech Lynx in Reutlingen. The large form of a flowing wave gathers all the functions under one roof. The form of the building reflects the dynamic work process and the corresponding corporate philosophy. Green communication areas run through the building structure constructed on maximum flexibility and provide a comfortable and creative working environment.

The front view reveals the total building construction. The facade corresponds to its contents. Like a large green wave, the building "rolls" down the hill, and opens itself in the direction of the city and the Alps. The topography is deliberately noticeably out and inside of the building. The "green wave" also reflects the hilly landscape in the Alps.

south facade with entrance | photo Roland Halbe

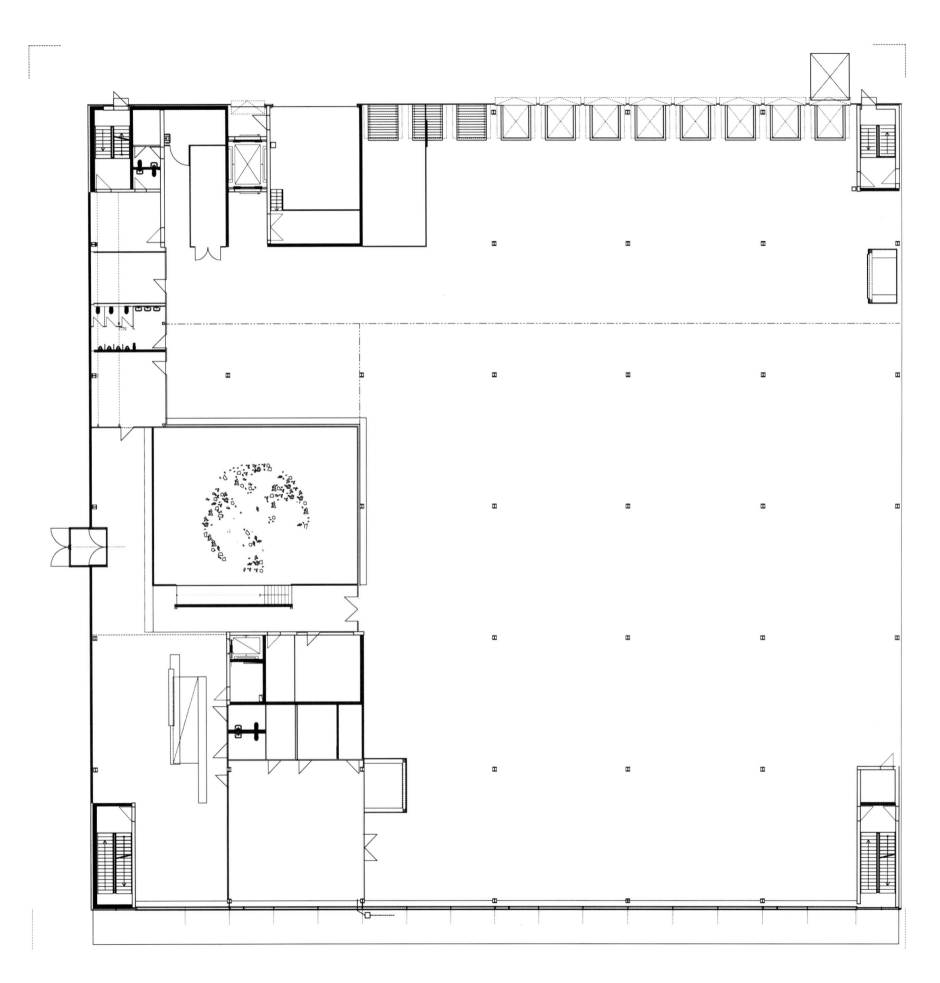

south facade | photo Roland Halbe

| courtyard | photo Roland Halbe |

void between office and production hall | photo Roland Halbe

INDUSTRIAL
SEMPERIT
NAJJAR & NAJJAR

Client:	Semperit Technische Produkte
Construction costs:	3 500 000 US Dollar
Work started:	2001
Completion:	2002
GFA:	2670 m²/ 28 729 m² ft
Use:	Building for Research and Development

Karim and Rames Najjar

The internationally successful company Semperit held a competition in 1999 for the design of a new research and development centre.

Najjar & Najjar's proposal for a metallic, shimmering building entitled "Tube" was chosen to represent the company's innovative profile.

The curved shape might be read as referring to the company's speciality, the forming of plastic and rubber. The laboratories on the ground floor are entirely glazed, and a sky-lit tube sits on top of them. In the centre is a hall poviding access to all areas. A slanted cut-off end functions as a glazed opening towards the busy road.

The refined aluminium surface of the dynamic volume suggests high production standards. In its perfectly slick appearance, it seems to imitate the bodywork of a sports car. Owing to this immaculate facade, and the consequent high quality realization from beginning to end, the project was awarded the Austrian Aluminium Award in 2002 and "Best Architects 07" award .

south elevation | photo Manfred Seidl

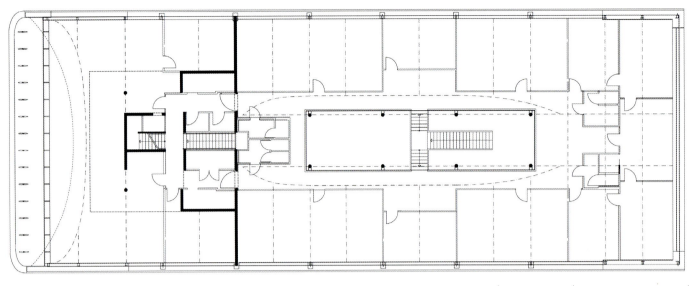

| ground plan | plan Najjar & Najjar |

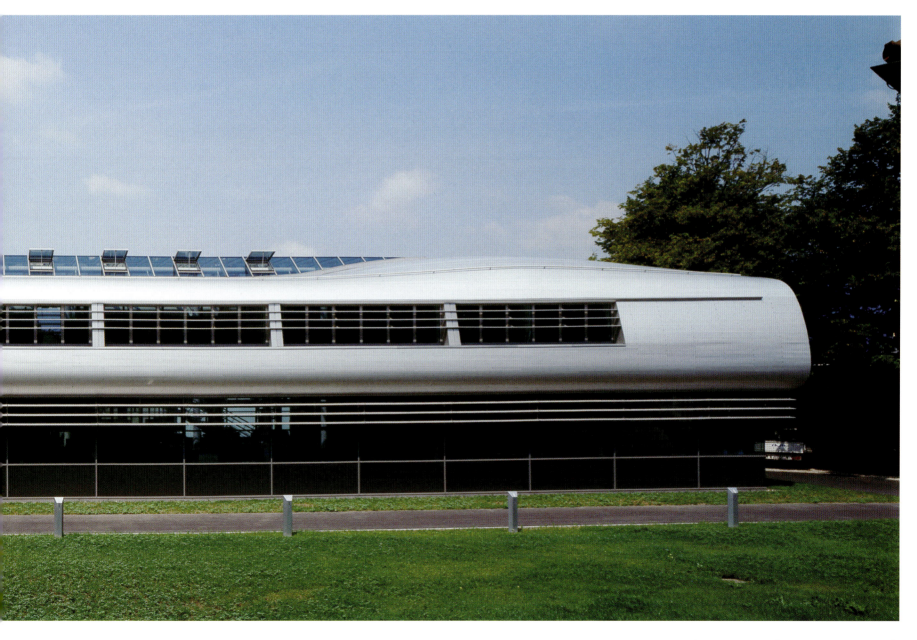

east elevation | photo Manfred Seidl | 087

| south-east view | photo Manfred Seidl |
| courtyard | photo Manfred Seidl |

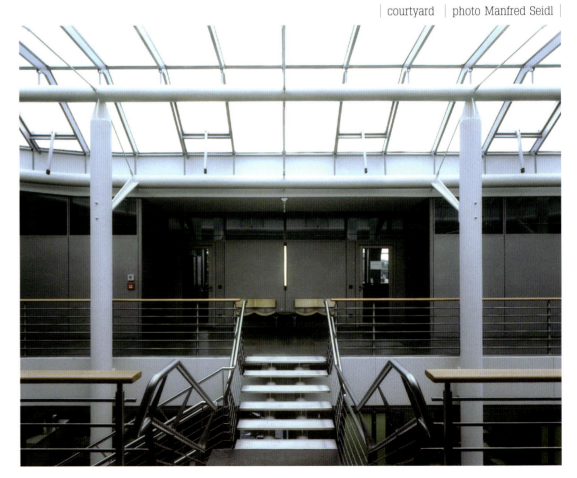

courtyard with staircase | photo Manfred Seidl

INDUSTRIAL
RE-TEM FACTORY
O.F.D.A.

Taku Sakaushi

Client:	Re-Tem Corporation (Recycle Technology & Management)
Completion:	4 / 2005
Location:	Ohta-ku, Tokyo, Japan
Site area:	5292.87 m²
Building area:	3994.14 m²

It was the project of the government of Tokyo to build a factory complex to promote the shift from mass consumption to recycling technology. Unlike other box-like buildings, the equipment is only partially concealed. In this way, the process of recycling is revealed.

The yard roof is ordered with a diagonal grid. As the oblique columns and beams work like a truss, the members become thin and light.

As for the office part, it is a symbol of this factory with a span of as long as 30 meters. It was modeled very intricately with polygon faces to form an organic shape. The wall of the second storey was cladded with numerous small pieces of glass to form a "double skin".

The glass skin is also patterned to create an effect of interference between these two patterns on the facade.

The effects of this new glass-cladding system were achieved without using expensive hi-tech details.

entrance facade | photo Hiroshi Ueda

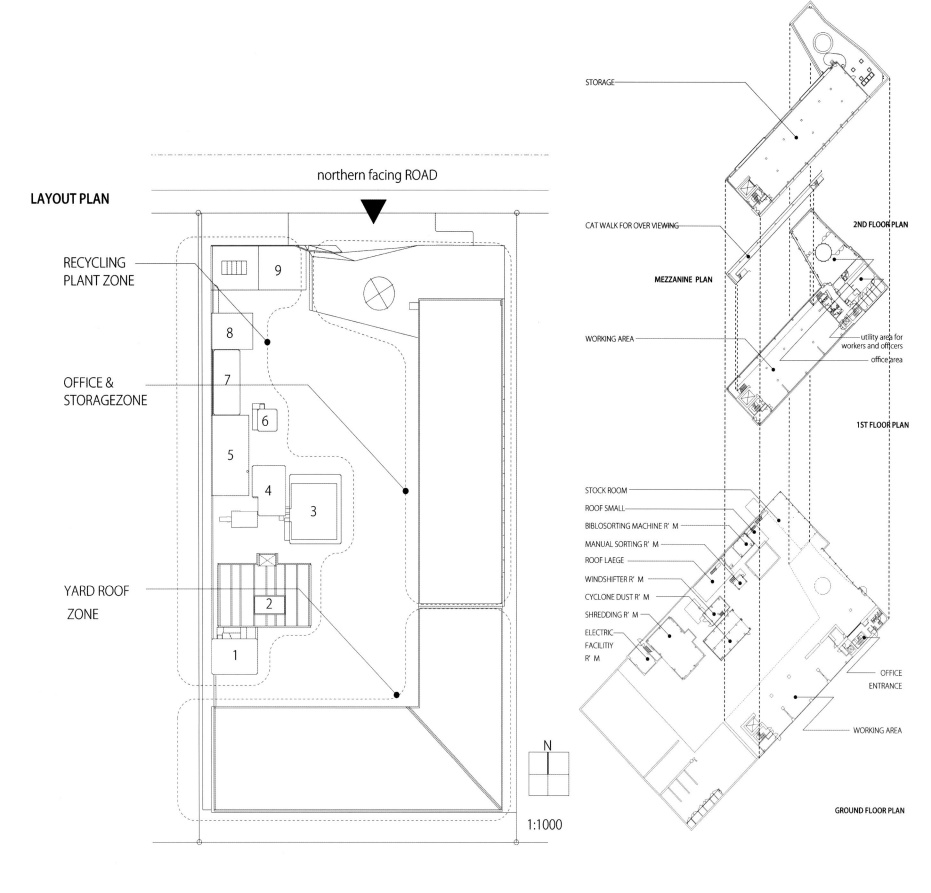

| site plan | plan O.F.D.A.

| north elevation | photo Hiroshi Ueda |
| courtyard view at night | photo Hiroshi Ueda |

| courtyard production line | photo Hiroshi Ueda |

| north facade | photo Hiroshi Ueda

INDUSTRIAL
VIT-INDUSTRIAL BUILDING ASPERHOFEN
QUERKRAFT ARCHITEKTEN

Client: VIT
Completion: 11 / 2003
Site: 2334 m²
Net effective area: 652 m²

In their design of an industrial building that caters to customers passing by on the highway, the architects proposed a simple steel pipe. This pipe lies on a slope, with parking space beneath it. Sited prominently and announcing its presence to the highway, it also offers a panoramic view of the valley. The discussion area and entrance are attached as a second generation of metal tubing, giving this industrial building its "loopy" characteristic.

An expressive construction attracts attention for this commercial firm. The heavily used main road becomes a "spectator's gallery". The underlying ground is only lightly touched by the building which hovers at the edge of the road. The entrance creates a threshold to the showroom – creating tension and setting the stage.

The intersection of simple and clear construction modules creates an unmistakeable object. The ingredients come from conventional industrial construction. Hovering above the slope allows the building to avoid expensive groundwork.

Jakob Dunkl   Gerd Erhartt   Peter Sapp

south-west view | photo Hertha Hurnaus

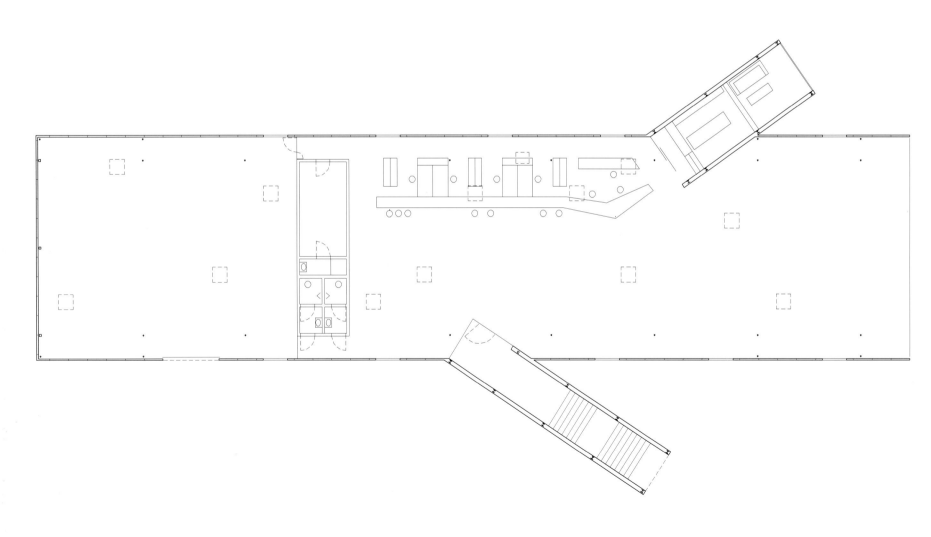

ground plan | plan Querkraft Architekten Zt Gmbh

south elevation | photo Hertha Hurnaus

| south-east view | photo Hertha Hurnaus |
| entrance at night | photo Hertha Hurnaus |

INDUSTRIAL
OTTEN FACTORY & OFFICE BUILDING
ARNO BREITER

Client:	Otten company
Completion:	1997
Total area:	5000 m²
Warehouse:	3000 m² (3 floors per 1000 m²)
Office:	1900 m²
Construction:	Roof and Walls - Steel, Steel-Sandwich panels Pillars and Floor - Concrete
Warehouse:	Concrete (prefabricated)
Office building:	Concrete

Arno Bereiter

The concept of the building was for the facade to reveal the dynamic movement of technology inside the factory, and the changing processes and machines.

The aerodynamic shape is for dissipating the hot air in the production space (because of the processes).

The building has four floors, all different in shape and layout. All spaces have to be flexible. All dividing walls can be changed and the main structure (concrete) is reduced to the minimum. To create a warm atmosphere for working, wood is the main material, in contrast to concrete. The rough concrete walls and ceilings are painted with pastel colours.

south-west view | photo Arno Breiter

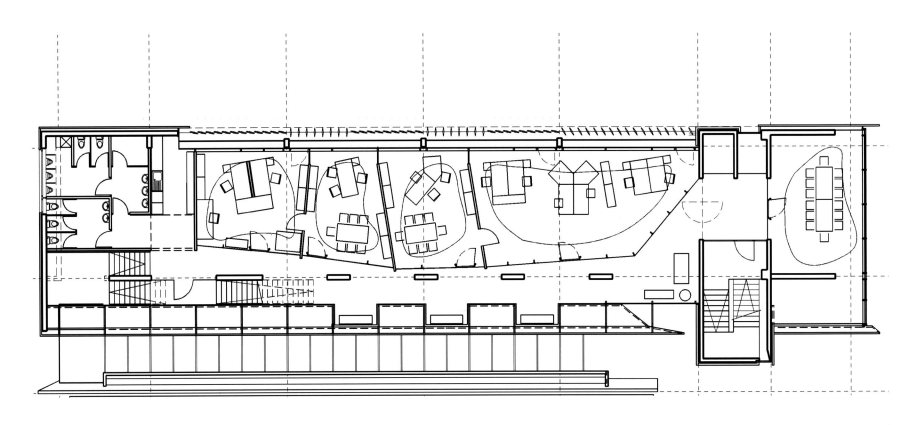

| ground plan | plan Arno Breiter |

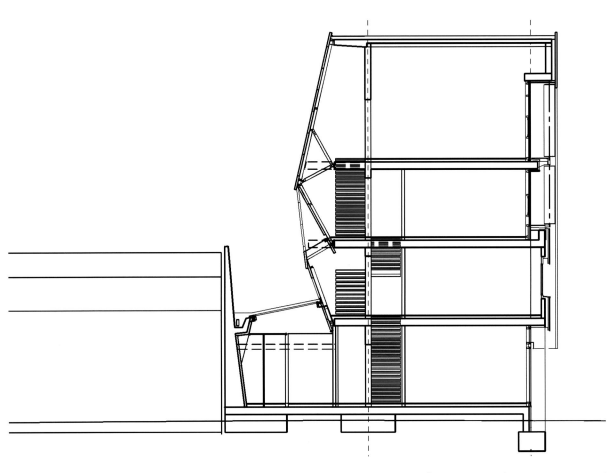

| section A-A | plan Arno Breiter |

| south elevation | photo Arno Breiter |
| factory facade | photo Arno Breiter |

| staircase view | photo Arno Breiter |

| office view | photo Arno Breiter |

| corridor | photo Arno Breiter |

INDUSTRIAL
PRINTING HOUSE CARINTHIA
ARCHITEKTUR CONSULT ZT GMBH

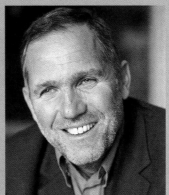

Domenig Eisenköck Peyker

Client:	Druck Carinthia GmbH & Co. KG
	St. Veit / Glan
Completion:	4 / 2003
Gross floor area:	6514 m²
Cost:	4.5 M.€

A new innovative object was created in the St. Veiter industrial park. The object's sculptured design is the distinguishing feature of the printing centre's unusual character.

An essential principle of the design is the compact, dynamic form of the structure, which was developed starting with its internal function and then projecting its activities together with their constant flow outwards.

The curved roof and the 20-meter-high rectangular tower allow the rapid work processes of the high-speed newspaper rotary printing press in the interior to be clearly conveyed to the outside. With the form of this structure Druck Carinthia GmbH & Co.KG communicates its very own corporate design.

The buildings of the printing house were planned in the extremely short period of only two months and erected within a period of twelve months.

south-west view | photo Paul Ott

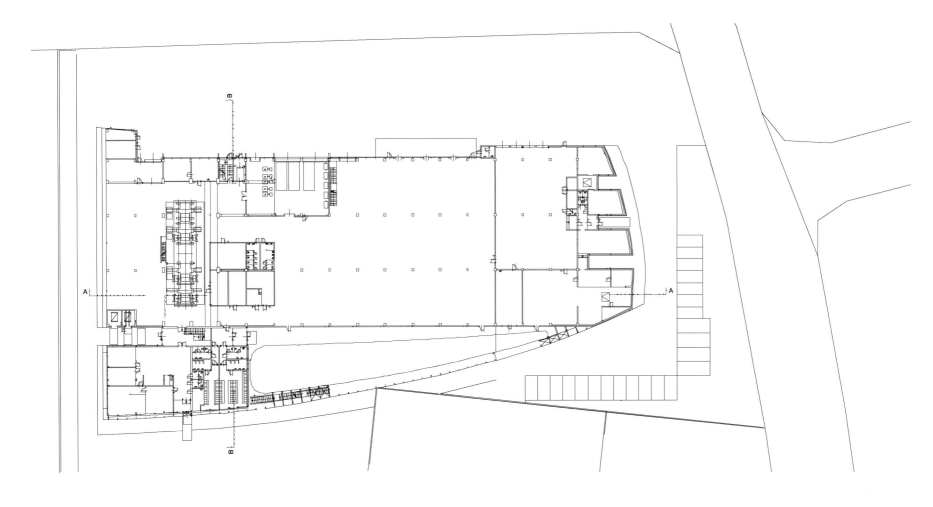

| ground plan | plan Architektur Consult ZT GmbH |

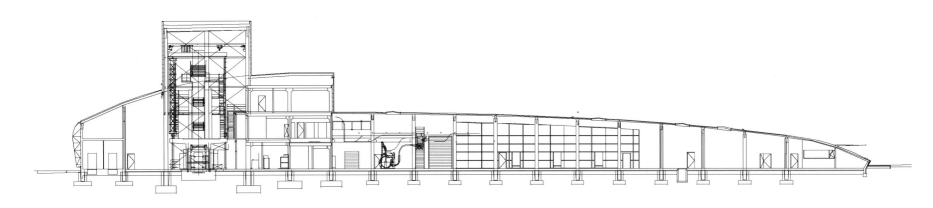

| longitudinal section | plan Architektur Consult ZT GmbH |

north-east view | photo Paul Ott

| south-east elevation | photo Paul Ott |
| north-west elevation | photo Paul Ott |

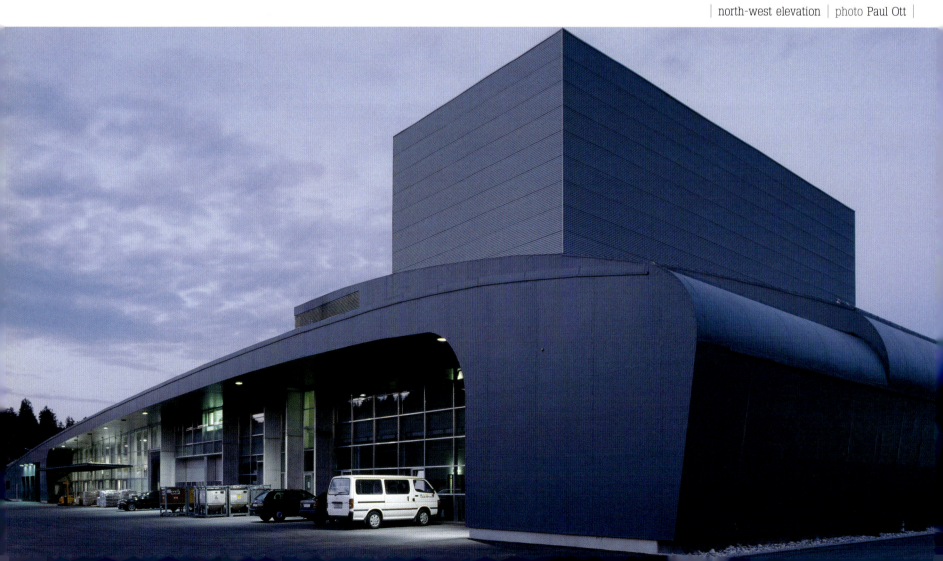

| south-west facade | photo Paul Ott |

INDUSTRIAL
NESPRESSO
BURCKHARDT + PARTNER AG

Client:	Nestlé SA, Orbe
Completion:	2003
Floor area:	9500 m²
Volume:	80 000 m³
Collaboration Partner:	Concept Consult Sárl

This building, with a volume of 125,000 cubic meters, focuses on transparency and the expression of the building envelope, comfort for users and industrial functionality. The visual appearance of the building complex is especially enhanced by the production structure. For the planners, building construction was characterized by the very high degree of necessary adaptability. As technologies and requirements change constantly, the main necessity was to ensure continuous flexibility in thinking and especially in the development of the construction site. Everything can be modulated, and the interior combines top architectural lighting quality with outstanding acoustics. Inside the production building, the selected colours that were specified for the equipment suppliers create a harmony often lacking in industrial buildings. In the sectors which may be extended at a later date, the walls are of a "hanging" design, allowing future removal and re-installation.

Philipp Brühlmeier

Peter Epting

Hans-Joerg Juchli

Roger Nussbaumer

Oliver Schmid

Samuel Schultze

west-south view | photo Pierre Boss

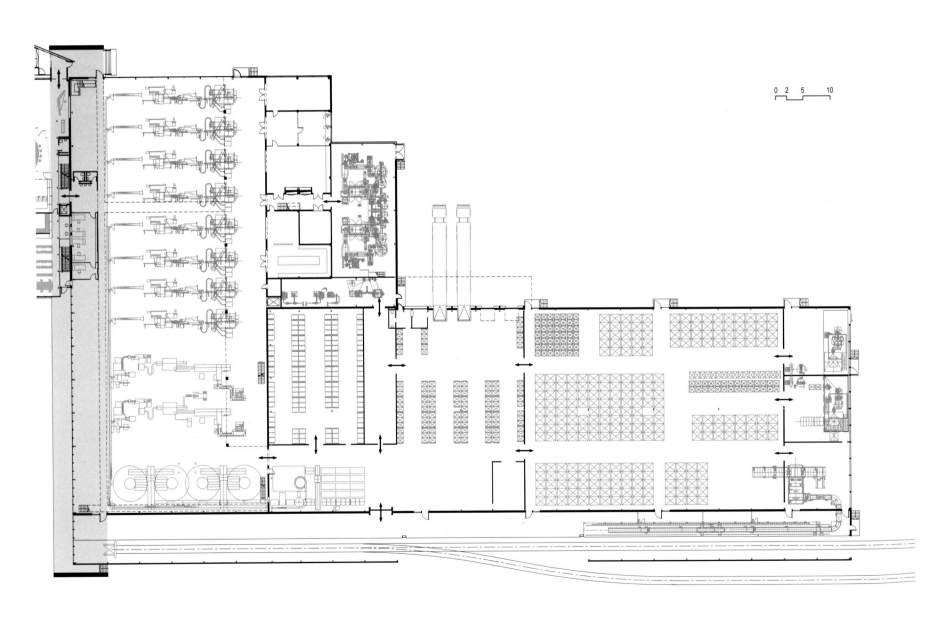

| ground plan | plan Burckhardt Partner AG |

west facade | photo Pierre Boss

| facade | photo Pierre Boss |
| production hall | photo Pierre Boss |

| logistic area | photo Pierre Boss |

INDUSTRIAL
ALPLA
FRÜH ARCHITEKTURBÜRO ZT GMBH

Alex Früh   Alex Fetz

Client:	Alpla Werke Hard
Completion:	2005
Value:	10 M.€
Production 1 area:	9200 m²
Production 2 area:	9400 m²
Store:	4500 m²
Office:	4500 m²

With its 74 000-cubic-meter volume, the dimension of the production hall is gigantic. But while the north facade inclines slightly and the building height slopes over the whole length from 14.7 meters to 13 meters, the building doesn't look oversized.

After three years of successful production, the second phase of construction has started. The expansion building, a tower-like office tract and the blow moulding department with the high rack warehouse are placed to surround – together with the old building – a courtyard, which shapes the new entrance situation.

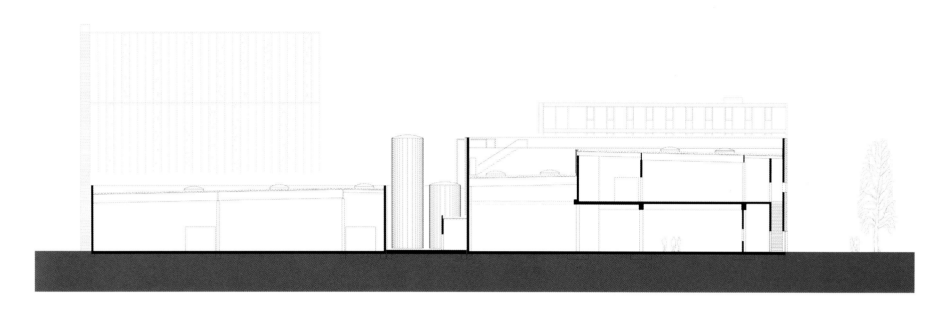

| section | plan FRÜH ARCHITEKTURbüro ZT GmbH |

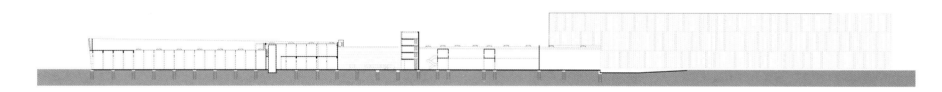

| longitudinal section | plan FRÜH ARCHITEKTURbüro ZT GmbH |

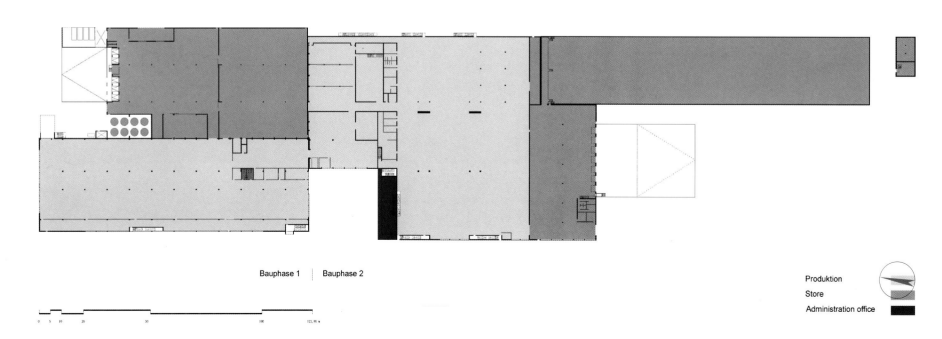

Bauphase 1 | Bauphase 2

Produktion
Store
Administration office

| ground plan | plan FRÜH ARCHITEKTURbüro ZT GmbH |

entrance | photo Adi Bereuter

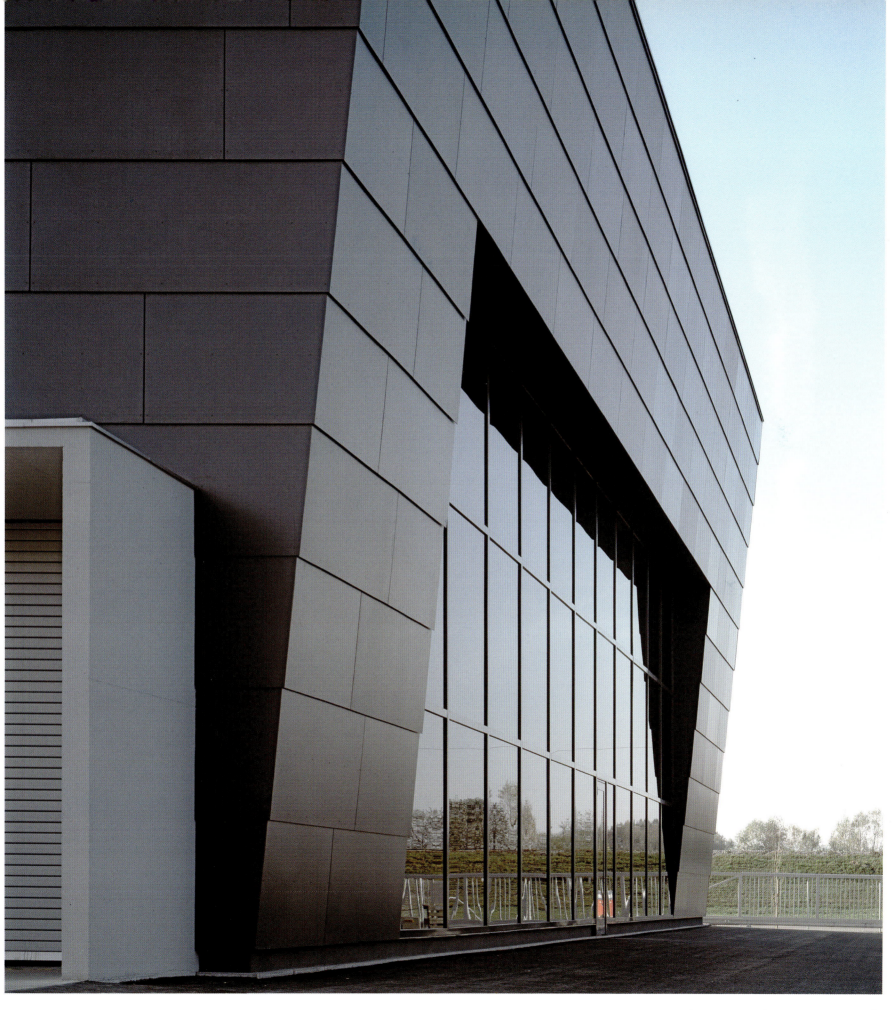

west facade | photo Adi Bereuter

PUBLIC
STADTHAUS
J. MAYER H.

J. Mayer H.

Client:	Cixy Ostfildern
Completion:	2002
Location:	Ostfildern, Germany
Structure:	steel-concrete building with aluminium facade
Site area:	1500 m²
Total floor area:	ca. 6000 m²

The Town Hall is located at the center of Scharnhauser Park, unifying various public services in one building. This combination of different programs generates synergetic effects provoking programmatic and visual transparency. From the main square to the panorama deck on the roof, the Town Hall interlocks with its context through cut-outs and terraces. These open air spaces remain accessible beyond the main opening hours and therefore serve as spatial and programmatic extensions. Light and water animations are an integral part of the Town Hall and induce subtle relationships between nature and technology. Framing the main entrance, visitors will have to walk through a computer animated artifical rain dripping from underneath the lit, flat cantilevered roof. On the square, suspended strings of light project a grid of lit spots onto the ground which is animated by the wind. Built-in webcams broadcast the moving images to the Town Hall and to the website of the city of Ostfildern. The Town Hall and the square construct a new public building prototype by offering simultaneity of city life in real, mediated and virtual space.

| north elevation | photo David Franck |

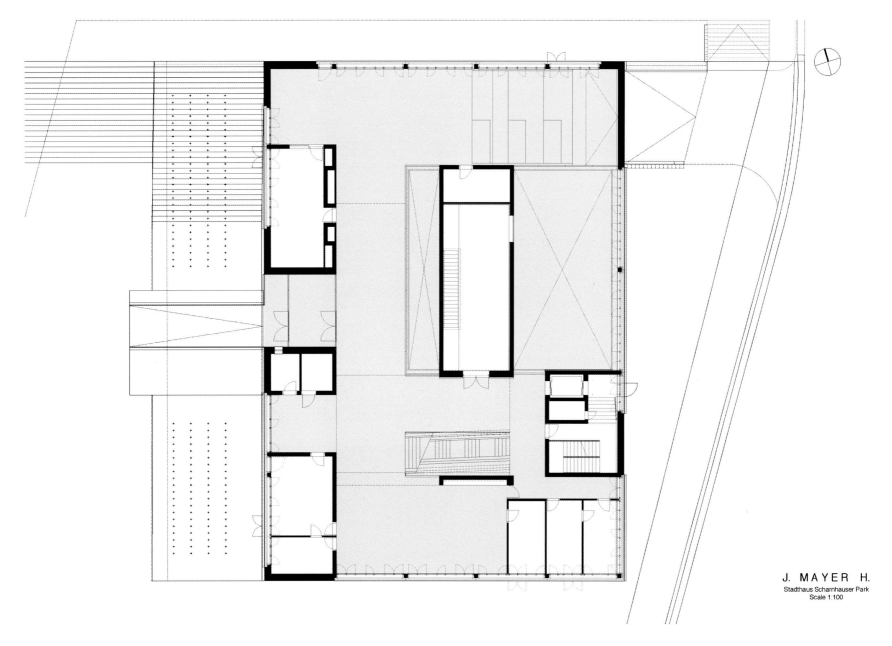

| ground plan | plan J. Mayer H. |

| south-west view | photo David Franck |

| hall | photo David Franck |

| entrance ensemble | photo David Franck |

| staircase | photo David Franck |

PUBLIC
JR SAITAMA STATION
EDWARD SUZUKI ASSOCIATION INC.

Edward Suzuki

Client:	JR East Japan
Completion:	6 / 2000
Location:	Saitama City
Site area:	7125.00 m²
Floor area:	5545.30 m²

This station was designed and built to become the gateway to the newly formed City of Saitama by the combination of previously existing cites of Ohmiya, Yono, and Urawa. As many new facilities with distinctive characters and features were expected to be built around the new station, a design that would naturally and harmoniously blend into the context of such was proposed in the form of a "formless" flowing cloud. In order to accommodate a peak crowd of spectators to and from the adjacent sports and cultural arena, a 23-meter clear span of a pedestrian deck promenade had to be housed and supplied within the station architecture. To satisfy this program need, an elliptical tunnel section was conceived to span the width of the promenade most efficiently. Where openings were needed to allow access to the station concourse, a part of this ellipse was simply opened up and supported by tree-like columns. The roof thus created continued on down the stairs to the platforms as a succession of waves. Parts of this roof were elevated at different heights to allow cross-ventilation throughout the station complex. Moreover, a third of this monolithic roof was made of transparent glass to provide ample natural light onto the station such that in days of sunshine one could watch a play of light and shadow on the floors throughout.

west view | photo Katsuaki Furudate

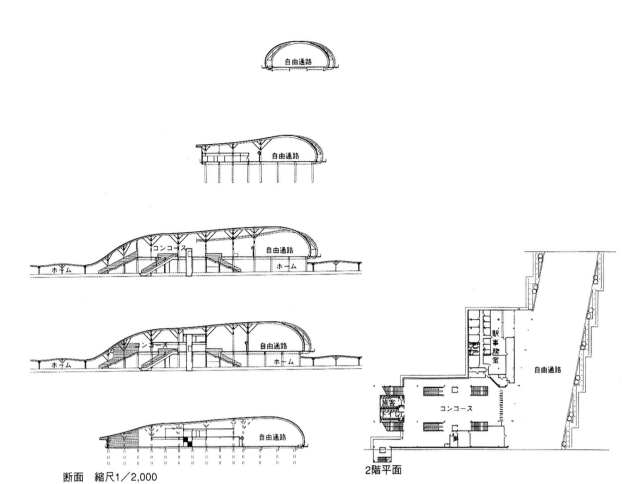

断面 縮尺1/2,000

| sections | plan Suzuki Association INC |

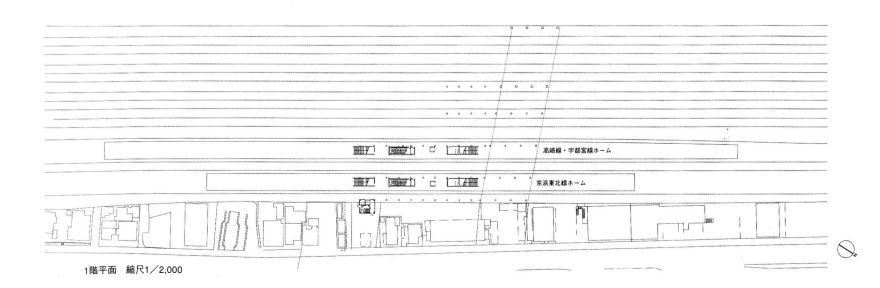

1階平面 縮尺1/2,000

| site plan | plan Suzuki Association INC |

east-west promenade | photo Katsuaki Furudate

| east-west promenade | photo Katsuaki Furudate |

PUBLIC
FESTHALLE WEISSACH
PETER W. SCHMIDT ARCHITEKT BDA

Client: Weissach, Rathausplatz 1, 71287 Weissach
Completion: 2005
Location: Flachter Straße 60, 71287 Weissach
Site area: 8350 m²
Floor area: 3296 m²

The festival hall of Weissach is embedded within the picturesque Strudelbach Valley. Through its slightly raised position, it becomes a Belvedere, whose views of the landscape are rendered part of the architecture. By directing the view into the valley, the inner courtyard between the hall and the restaurant points to the contrast between architecture and nature and its tectonic walls frame the threshold to the landscape. Analogous to the reciprocal relationship between surroundings and the festival hall, the building's elements are complexly linked together. The northern end of the horizontally aligned stone base is turned vertically forming the backbone of the hall. It becomes the counterpart to the filigree roof, which seems to float above the building. A vitreous volume is clamped in between these two elements, which is sometimes offset, forming generous covered balconies. These communication spaces represent the archetype of the loggia and refer to the classical traditions of architecture.

Peter W. Schmidt

| east elevation | photo Stefan Müller

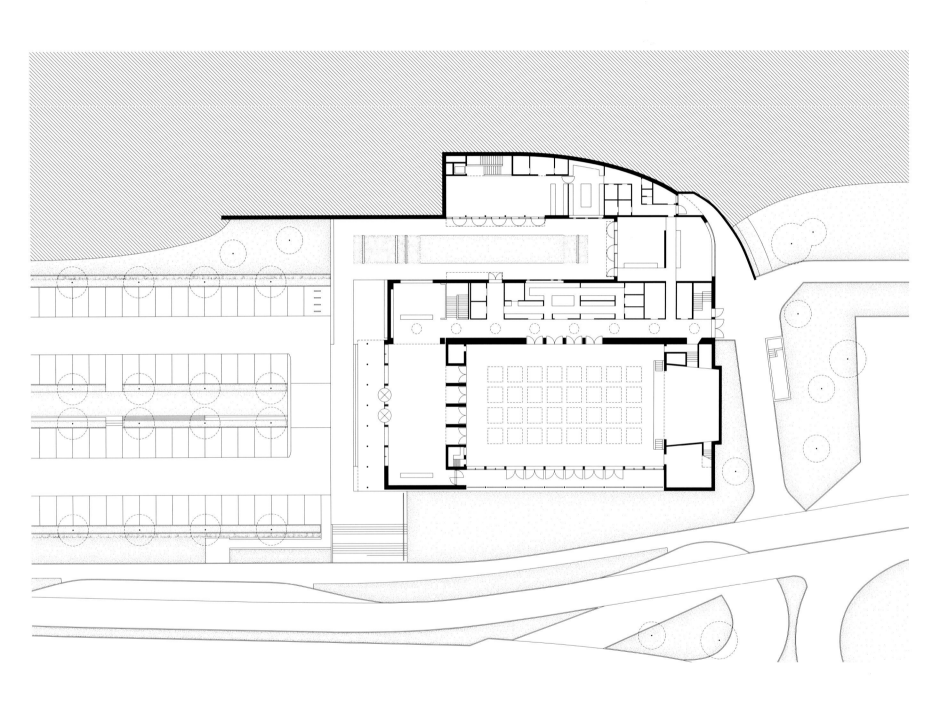

| site plan | plan Peter W. Schmidt Architekt BDA |

south-east view | photo Stefan Müller

| multifunctional hall | photo Stefan Müller |
| foyer | photo Stefan Müller |

| south elevation | photo Stefan Müller |

PUBLIC
BUBBLETECTURE M
ENDO SHUHEI

Endo Shuhei

Client:	Maihara City
Completion:	5 / 2003
Location:	Maihara City, Shiga Pref.
Structure:	Wood + RC
Site area:	3987 m²
Floor area:	1398 m²

The architects realized this project taking two important ideas into consideration. One is that the required spaces for children cannot be limited by a planner. Instead, these spaces should be visualized by children with their imaginations. The space for children is covered with one continuous roof.

This opened space allows children to play freely. The corridor between classroom and playground is assumed as intermediated space. The architects expect that this ambiguity of the space will stimulate children's imaginations.

The other idea is the adaptation of the material that composes the space. Materials have to be selected for their health and safety because children touch them directly. The architects adapted natural wood instead of using laminated wood. Attention was paid not only to the materials of walls and floors but also to the materials of furniture such as chairs and tables for children's health.

A new structure system was proposed using natural wood to realize the space of timber structure for children. The structure system uses wooden beams and hexagonal metal fittings to allow various geometrical forms. The metal fittings are treated in such a way that these form 284 different parts.

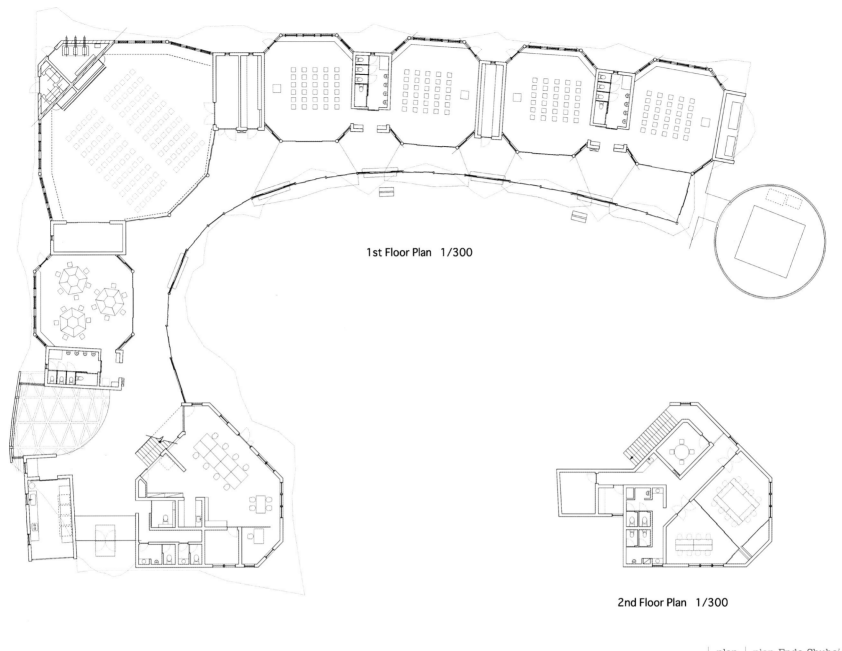

1st Floor Plan 1/300

2nd Floor Plan 1/300

| plan | plan Endo Shuhei |

SOUTH ELEVATION 1/300

NORTH ELEVATION 1/300

| north and south elevations | plan Endo Shuhei |

| multifunctional room | photo Yoshiharu Matsumura |
| foyer area | photo Yoshiharu Matsumura |

west elevation | photo Yoshiharu Matsumura

PUBLIC
SURUGA KINDERGARTEN
O.F.D.A.

Taku Sakaushi

Client: Kawai-gakuen
Architect: Taku Sakaushi
Chika Kijima
Completion: 2005
Location: Shizuoka Pref., Japan.
Site area: 2857 m²
Building area: 1295 m²
Floor area: 2516 m²

There were three kindergarten buildings on the site. Among them, the middle one was the oldest and it was planned to be rebuilt.

Each floor of this building has a long corridor with four classrooms beside, and each one is also connected to the other building of the kindergarten complex. The architects' answer to avoid wind and rain was quite simple; a rain-proof screen. So the idea of this light corridor in front of the building became the core concept of this project.

The screen has to release heat and also illuminate the classrooms from the garden. The material choice was an important solution to fulfil the requirements of the concept. The architects finally decided to use the thick poly-carbonate panels made in Germany because of the durability and safety.

The dry light corridors ensure that the space is not too hot, not too cold, and not too closed. Pupils and teachers can enjoy the interesting view of the garden through the various shapes of the holes.

| south elevation | photo Hiroshi Ueda |

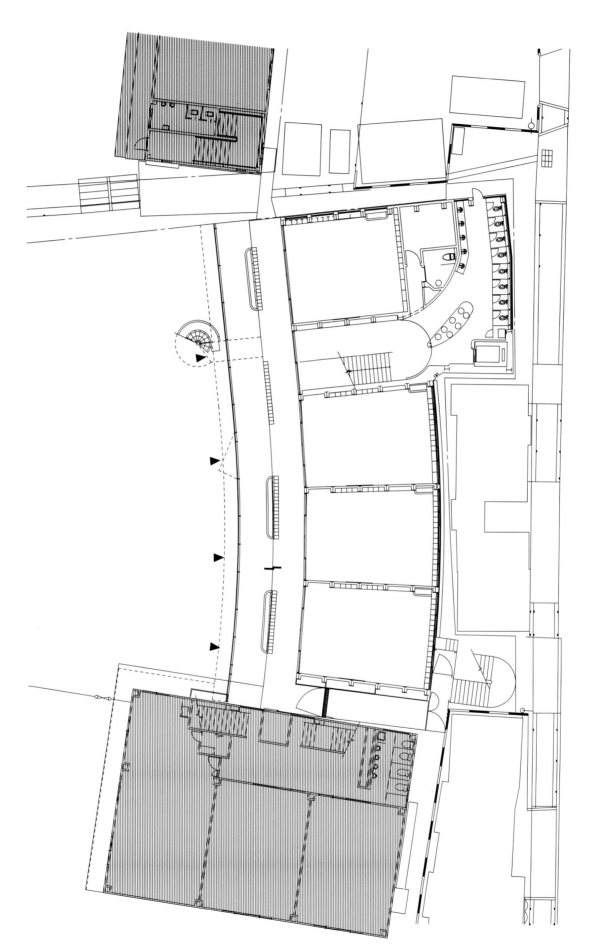

ground plan | plan O.F.D.A.

south facade | photo Hiroshi Ueda

| multifuctional room | photo Hiroshi Ueda |

| corridor | photo Hiroshi Ueda |

| open air washing area | photo Hiroshi Ueda |

HOUSING
EDDI'S HOUSE
EDWARD SUZUKI ASSOCIATION INC.

Edward Suzuki

Client: Daiwa House Industry
Completion: 2002
Location: Nara City
Structure: Light Weight Steel, 2 Stories
Site area: 297.00 m²
Floor area: 144.43 m²

This is a prefabricated housing system developed in collaboration with Daiwa House Kogyo, a major housing manufacturer in Japan. EDDI stands for Edward Daiwa Design Innovation. The concept of the house is "Go in to go out." Being an industrialized housing system designed without knowing the future user of the house, it was assumed from previous experiences that the context in which the house is to built could not be counted upon as being favorable. Hence, the house was designed basically to be inward-looking towards a patio, whether outdoor or indoor, depending on the house type.

Futhermore, a balcony is placed above and adjacent to the central patio overlooking it such that this combination of open spaces creates an "interface" between the outside proper and the inside that acts as a filter, a buffer, or a cushion between the two zones. In this way, the design is such that the house does not need to depend on the contextual conditions in which it is to be situated. No matter how unfavorable the surroudings may be, the house would function comfortably within the mini-cosmos of its own boundaries.

south elevation | photo Daishin-shya

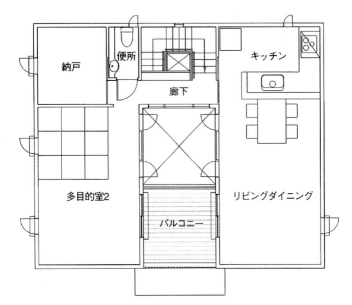

2階平面

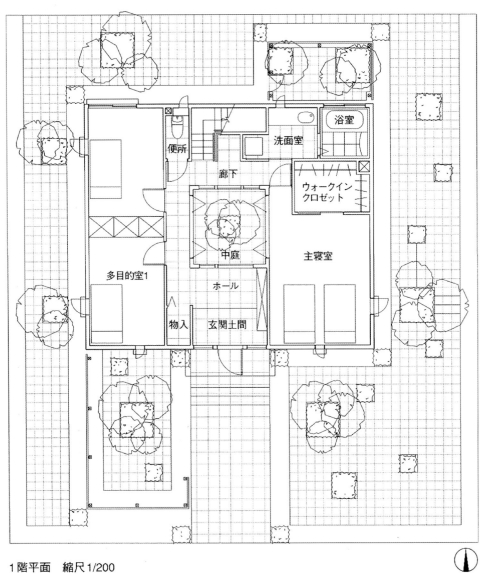

1階平面　縮尺1/200

| south-east view at night | photo Daishin-shya |

| bed room | photo Daishin-shya |

| terrace | photo Daishin-shya |

| courtyard view | photo Daishin-shya |

HOUSING
C+R GRABHER HOUSE
ARNO BEREITER

Arno Bereiter

Client:	Carmen and Ralph Grabher
Completion:	2003
Location:	Lustenau, Staldenstrasse, Austria
Structure:	Floors and walls – concrete
	Roofs – wood and Eternit
Site area:	1050 m²
Floor area:	175 m²

The residence comprises two structures. The tower is much less defined by its height (13.8 meters) but more through its slender proportions, containing three bedrooms with bathroom. The main functions of the house are arranged to be flexible, the kitchen to be portable, and the living room to open onto three differently orientated and enclosed terraces. Depending of the time of the day and year, the inhabitant can follow the movement of the sun by moving from one place to the other. A carport and a work area are attached to the main structure. The main design concept is further reinforced through the broad range and natural use of materials in the house. It is the intention to create a house which completes itself through the inhabitant as opposed to creating a designer-focused house that welcomes its new inhabitant as an intruder.

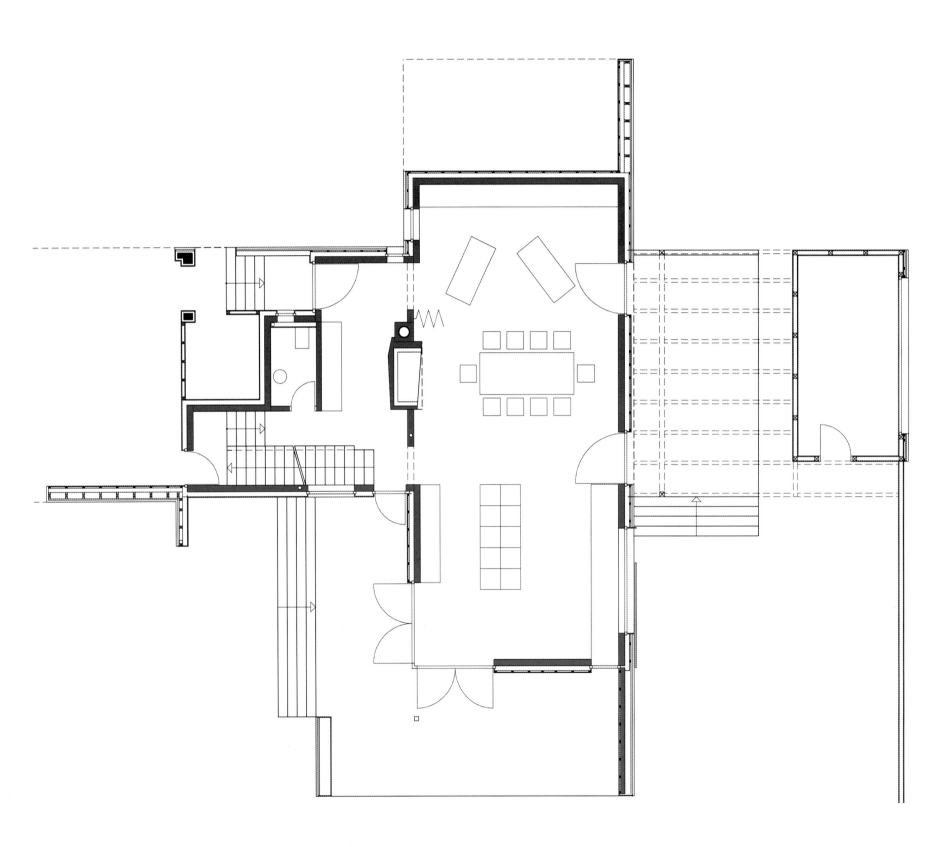

ground plan | plan Arno Bereiter

north elevation | photo Albrecht Schnabel

| west elevation | photo Albrecht Schnabel |
| terrace | photo Albrecht Schnabel |

east elevation | photo Albrecht Schnabel

HOUSING
RESIDENCE KLOSTERNEUBURG
PROJECT A01 ARCHITECTS

Client: Private
Completion: 4 / 2006
Location: Klosterneuburg, near Vienna
Structure: Concrete; Steel columns
Site area: 3418 m²
Total floor area: 470 m²

Team Project A01

This spacious mansion for a young family in Klosterneuburg near Vienna was completed in May 2006.

Situated on a hill overlooking the whole valley, the base of the building roughly follows the slope and is slightly terraced in itself. Following this concept, the ground floor consists of several levels, which divide the lavish loft-like living space into various functional areas like the fireplace, lounge and dining area, kitchen and breakfast terrace. Various patios and terraces as well as a swimming pool are arranged around the building and create a seamless connection between the living space indoors and the landscape outdoors. A cantilevered structure housing the family's private rooms is located floating above the ground floor being carried by slender steel columns. The rooftop terrace in front of the master bedroom offers a grand view over the green valley scenery.

south-west elevation | photo Andreas Schmitzer

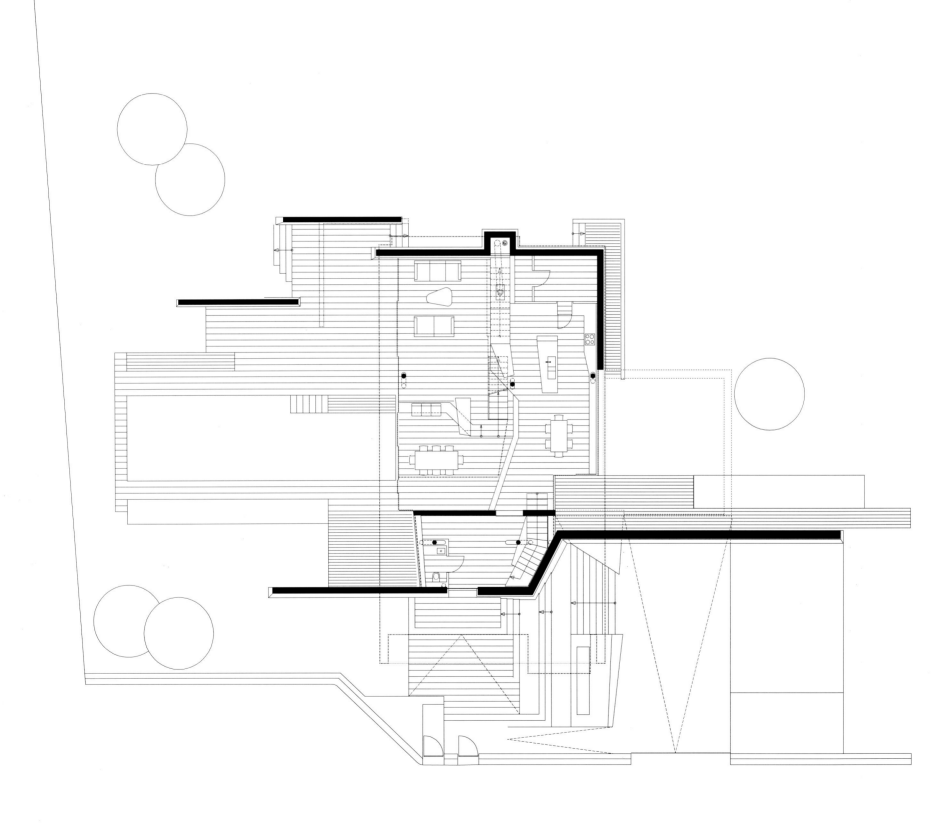

| ground plan | plan Project A01 Architects |

west elevation at night | photo Andreas Schmitzer

| kitchen area | photo Andreas Schmitzer |

south elevation | photo Andreas Schmitzer

HOUSING
HOUSE IN BISHAMON
SUPPOSE DESIGN OFFICE

Makoto Tanijiri

Completion: 4 / 2003
Location: Bishamon Hirosima JPN
Structure: ferroconcrete with iron frames, 3 storied
Plot area: 710.59 m²
Building area: 80.20 m²
Total floor area: 189.88 m²

The Bishamon float is a house with a cafe located on a hill in Hiroshima city and built for two family members and a dog. Many stereotypical houses built by well-known Japanese developers surround the Bishamon float, but only this lot has greenery, or the "power of nature" on both sides.

By putting two pairs of slabs and a light roof on six poles which look like iron frames of a swing, the floating box of the Bishamon float building was completed.

The first floor is a cafe run by the owner of the building and the second floor with a unique bridge is the family's space where the architects designed a bathroom and kitchen in the center of the room. They tried to create an open and comfortable space on the second floor by taking advantage of the soft sunlight on the leaves of trees and luminous lights under the building. This is a simple but dynamic structure that gives building design a new and remarkable phase.

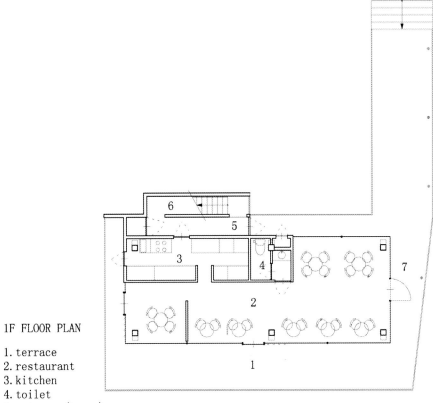

1F FLOOR PLAN

1. terrace
2. restaurant
3. kitchen
4. toilet
5. entrance (house)
6. closet
7. entrance (restaurant)

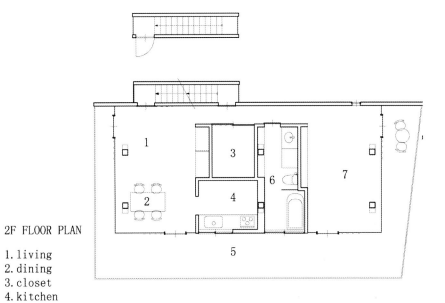

2F FLOOR PLAN

1. living
2. dining
3. closet
4. kitchen
5. terrace
6. lavatory / bath room
7. bed room

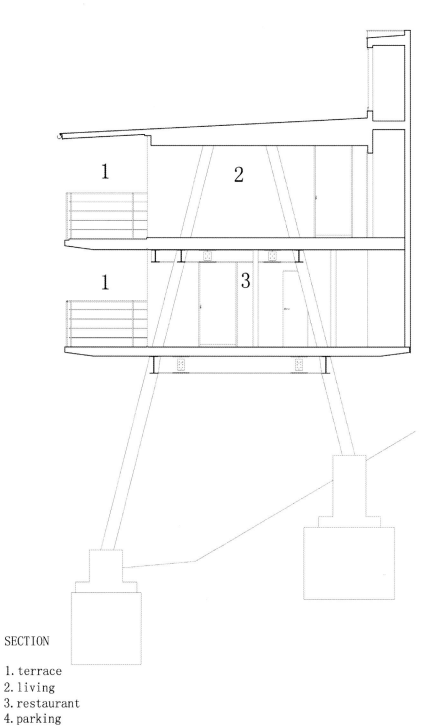

SECTION

1. terrace
2. living
3. restaurant
4. parking

north-east view | photo Nacasa & Partners

| west elevation | photo Nacasa & Partners

| entrance situation | photo Nacasa & Partners |

| living area | photo Nacasa & Partners |

HOUSING
SINGLE FAMILY HOUSE IN GAUTING
ABP ARCHITEKTEN

Client:	Gisela and Alexander Guentsch
Completion:	01 / 2003
Location:	Ulmenstrasse 13, D-82131 Gauting
Structure:	Timber-Framed Construction
Site area:	524 m²
Floor area:	151 m²

Thomas Pfeiffer

Edgar Burian

The outer appearance of this small timber-framed building shows two quite different sides. Towards the street the façade is rather closed and homogeneous. Covered with rough larch-wood strips, the windows can be shut by sliding shutters made of the same material. On the opposite side, there are big sliding windows opening the interior of the house onto the garden. Here, the terrace is conceived as a cut out. The inner facade of this cut is lined with a fine, furniture-like surface. The terrace and the one sided roof are marking a fluent transition from the inside to the outside.

The heart of the house is the large cooking and eating zone. Situated in the middle of this area, the stairway is not only the access to the second floor but also part of the living area. It connects the two levels inside with an open space and leads onto the upper landing which is illuminated by a big frameless window at the rooftop. This place is the access to the bedrooms but also used for children's play and working space. The continuity of the spaces and the multifunctionality of their use give this small economical building a touch of generosity.

south elevation | photo ABP Architekten

ground plan | plan ABP Architekten

| staircase and terrace | photo ABP Architekten |

| north elevation | photo ABP Architekten |

| entrance | photo ABP Architekten |

| terrace | photo ABP Architekten |

HOUSING
FISCHER-STEGEN RESIDENCE
PICHLER & TRAUPMANN

Christoph Pichler Johann Traupmann

Client: Dr. Ina Stegen, Dr. Helmut Fischer
Completion: 2003
Location: Salzburg, Austria
Structure: Concrete
Site area: 1184 m²
Floor area: 445 m²

The clients, two art collectors, owned a lot very close to the city of Salzburg with a spectacular view towards the Salzburg Castle. Their brief asked for a house providing generous spaces for working, living and hosting guests.

The house consists of seven inter-connected levels, whose continuous space is achieved through a complex system of spatial volumes of different ceiling heights. One enters either at the lowest level, the carport-level, or at the entrance-level via a set of outdoor stairs. The spa area is located between these two levels. From the library, sleeping level and a gallery one finally reaches the dining and living area which hovers above the building to allow an uninterrupted view of the city and its castle. All seven levels open to the outside, either to the garden, terraces or roof terraces.

The site is characterized by a very special topography. It has a very steep slope in the form of a quarter of a bowl. Thus, at the lot's perimeter, the slope falls in two directions orthogonally to one other. These two axes became crucial for the design and organization of the building for one exactly follows the view axis towards the castle. This axis serves as the virtual connection of the building and its levels with the city, whereas the other axis serves as an actual connection with the site and the levels themselves by a system of outdoor and indoor stairs and ramps. Whenever one walks on them one follows the direction inherent in the site, whenever one turns one is overwhelmed by the view of the city and castle.

| south elevation | photo Andrew Phelps

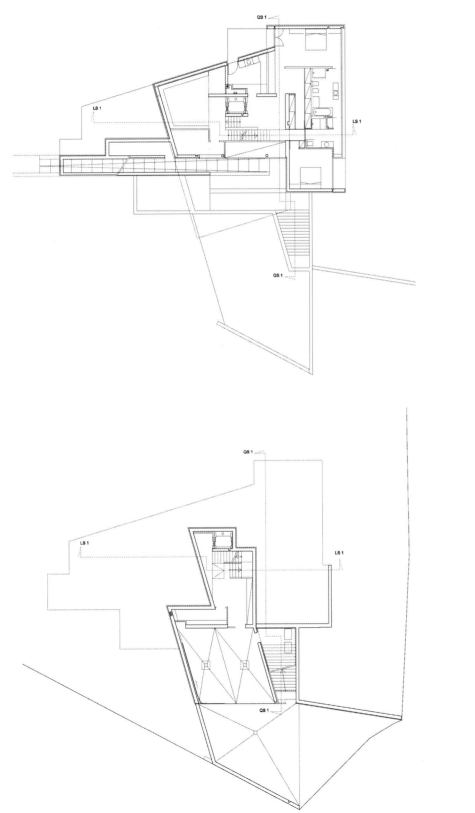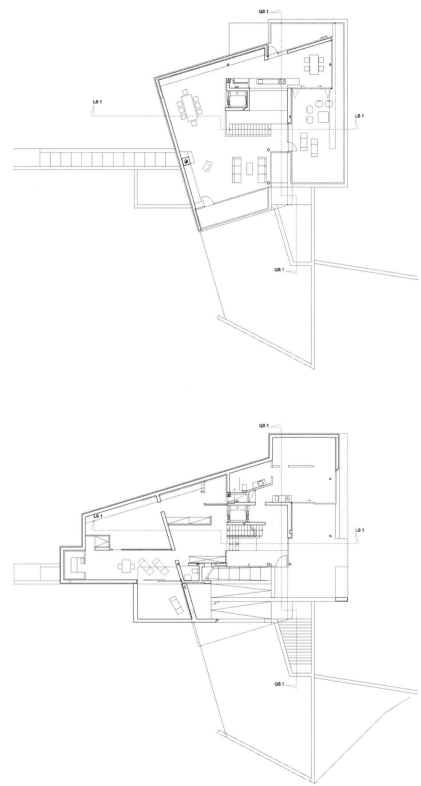

| ground plans | plan Pichler & Traupmann |

east view | photo Andrew Phelps

| staircase | photo Andrew Phelps |

void between terrace and living | photo Andrew Phelps

terrace | photo Andrew Phelps

RESIDENTIAL
SEEWUERFEL
CAMENZIND EVOLUTION

Client:	Swiss Life
Completion:	5 / 2005
Location:	Seefeldstrasse 277, 8008 Zurich, Switzerland
Structure:	Concrete / Steel
Site area:	5270 m²
Floor area:	11 950 m²

Stefan Camenzind   Tanya Ruegg-Basheva   Nicole Buschor

The eight new apartment and office buildings are situated close to the town centre of Zurich and offer stunning views of the lake and surrounding cityscape. The project regenerates a former industrial site into a new attractive centre for working and living and integrates itself harmoniously into the existing historic fabric of the area. The project was awarded the RIBA World-Wide Award 2005 by the Royal Institute of British Architects.

The exceptional quality of the project lies in the balance achieved between the unique modern architectural language of the development, the individual identity given to buildings by avoiding uniformity and the harmonious way in which the project integrates into the historic fabric of the neighborhood.

The lower three floors of each building contain office space and the upper two floors are used for luxurious maisonette apartments. To give the buildings their own individuality and unique identity within the Seewurfel development, CamenzindEvolution specifically developed a new silicon-bonded timber-glass-panel cladding system.

south-west view | photo Camenzind Evolution

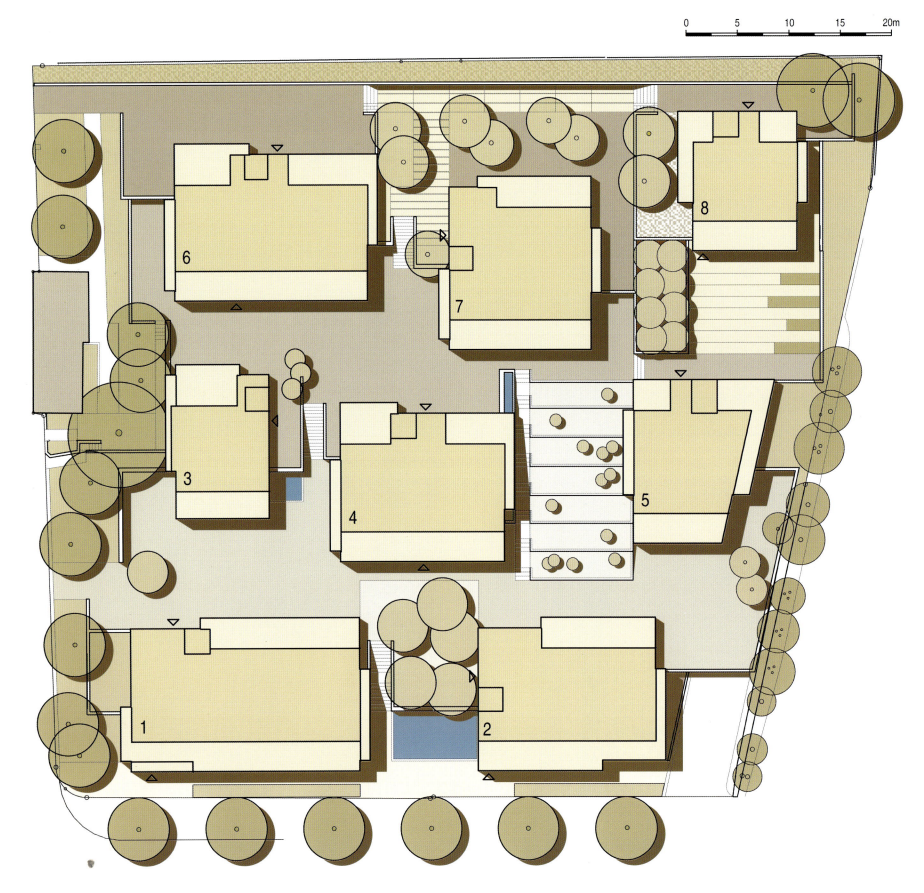

| site plan | plan Camenzind Evolution |

courtyard view | photo Camenzind Evolution

| east elevation | photo Camenzind Evolution |

| courtyard | photo Camenzind Evolution |
| bath room view | photo Camenzind Evolution |

RESIDENTIAL MONTEVIDEO
MECANOO ARCHITECTEN

Francine Houben

Client: ING Real Estate, The Hague
Completion: 2003-2005
Architect: Francine Houben
Mecanoo architecten bv, Delft
GFA: 57 530 m²
of which 36 867 m² residential;
905 m² swimming pool;
fitness and service centre;
6129 m² offices;
1608 m² retail;
8413 m² car park

Montevideo consists of a composition of intersecting volumes, part of which is suspended above the quay. The building refers to the high-rise buildings of New York, Chicago and Boston: brick-built, with refined detailing and use of colour, a lot of roof terraces and loggias. The construction contributes to the Holland-America feeling: a system that alternates steel (America) with concrete (Holland). The first two floors are built of steel and bear the 152-meter-high tower and the Water Apartments jutting 16 meters out. The 27 floors above are executed with a concrete climbing form. From the 28th floor steel is used, so that the floors of these apartments are freely subdivisible. This allows the building to achieve a very varied spatial structure: 192 dwellings with no less than 54 different types and different floor heights divided amongst Loft, City, Sky and Water apartments. All this on top of a two-story underground parking facility. Windows, balconies and loggias are distributed across the building in a rhythmic composition: corner-spanning, story-high, circular, staggered, opening on hinges and sliding open. The diagonals of the steel construction of the top floors can be described through the windows.

south-east facade | photo Christian Richters

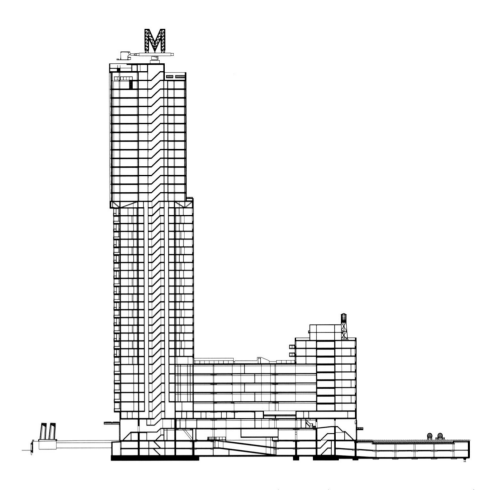

| section | plan Mecanoo Architecten |

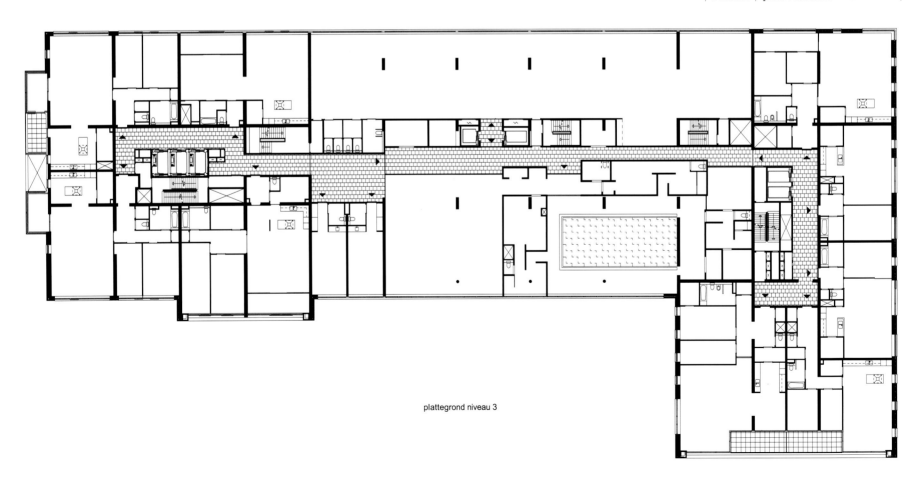

plattegrond niveau 3

| ground plan-level 3 | plan Mecanoo Architecten |

south west facade | photo Christian Richters

| entrance lobby tower | photo Christian Richters |
| transparent plinth | photo Christian Richters |

RESIDENTIAL
KENYUEN
MURAMATSU ARCHITECTS

Motoyasu Muramatsu

Project name:	The evening of life on the ground between the Ocean and the sky text by Motoyasu Muramatsu
Location:	Susami-cho, Nishimuro-gun, Wakayama Japan
Total site area:	15 490 m²
Total built-up area:	4973 m²
Completion:	2001

The site is located on cliffs overlooking the Pacific Ocean with superb and unlimited views .

The expanded Z-shaped building lies on an axis from the mountains north to the sea south in order to harmonize with the uneven land. Alongside the building, the vast land is divided into a pair of L-shaped fields; one is the approach facing the mountains and the other is the garden facing the ocean. At once, transparent space has been created in the middle of the building, to produce a sense of free spatial flow from the mountain to the ocean.

The architect's aim is to create architectural spaces, places and times that establish relationships between people and their environment, for people to better appreciate the changes in days and seasons, as well as the scenery surrounding them.

entrance ensemble | photo Nacasa & Partners

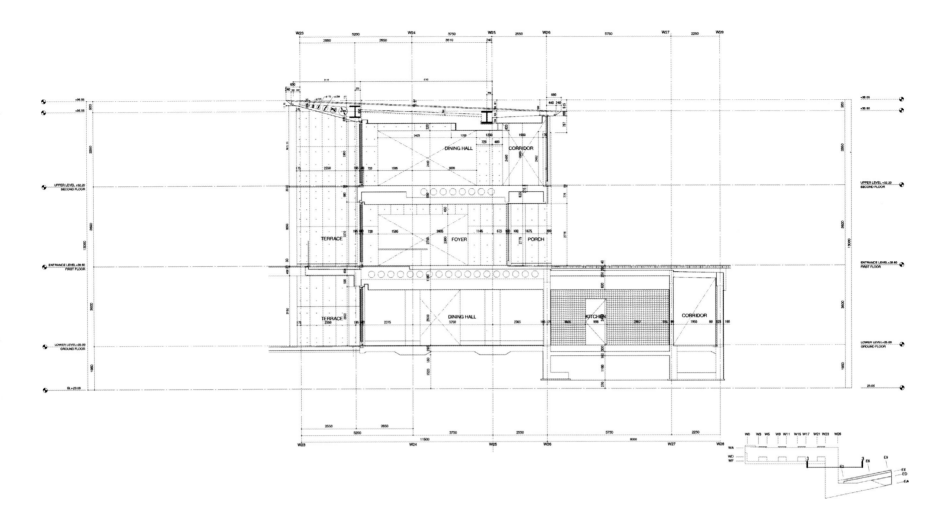

| section | plan Muramatsu Architects |

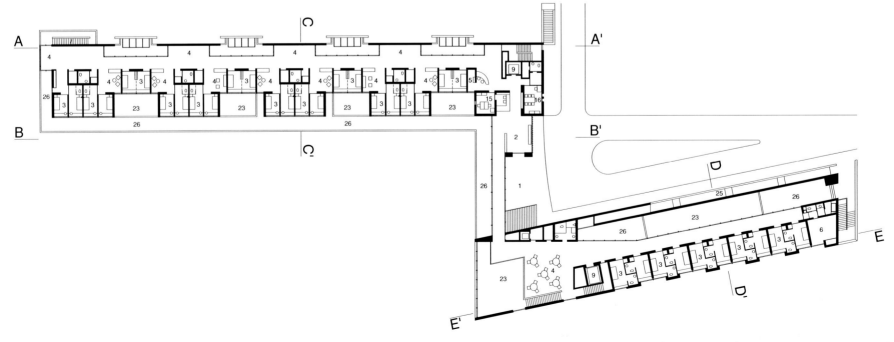

| ground plan | plan Muramatsu Architects |

| east facade | photo Nacasa & partners |

| west facade | photo Nacasa & Partners |
| corridor | photo Nacasa & partners |

pool for SPA therapy | photo Nacasa & partners

RESIDENTIAL
SPITTELAU VIADUCTS HOUSING
ZAHA HADID ARCHITECTS

Client:	SEG - Stadterneuerungs- und Eigentumswohnungsges.m.b.H
Cubage:	7980 m³
Building costs:	9.5 M.€
Completion:	12 / 2005

A series of apartments, offices and artist's studios weave like a ribbon through, around and over the arched bays of the viaduct, designed by Otto Wagner. The viaduct itself is a protected structure, and may not be interfered with. The three-part structure playfully interacts with the viaduct, generating a multitude of different outdoor and indoor spatial relationships. The perception of these is intensifed by the response of the architectural language to the different speeds of the infrastructural elements.

Public outdoor spaces are enlivened via the infill of bars and restaurants under the arches of the viaduct. The related service zone flows through the remaining openings of the viaduct and melts into the banks of the canal, creating a lively platform for public life. The rooftops are planned as private retreats and add to the visual activity along the canal. An additional challenge is posed to the project, as the program consists mainly of social housing, though studios and offices are mixed in. Later, the project should be connected to the University of Business and Northern Train Station via a pedestrian and cycle bridge.

Zaha Hadid   Portrait Steve Double

east elevation | photo Margherita Spiluttini

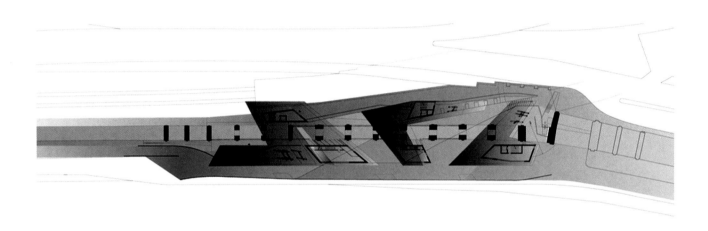

| ground plan | plan Zaha Hadid |

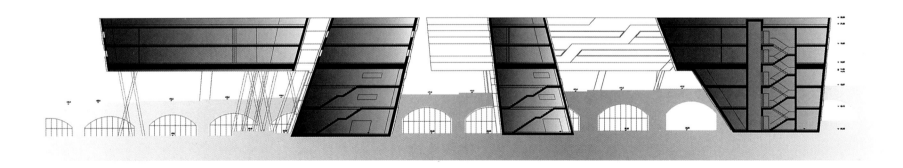

| section | plan Zaha Hadid |

| west elevation | photo Margherita Spiluttini |

| courtyard | photo Margherita Spiluttini |

 | east facade | photo Margherita Spiluttini |

 | west facade | photo Margherita Spiluttini |

RESIDENTIAL
RIVER HEIGHTS
GORDON MURRAY + ALAN DUNLOP

Alan Dunlop   Geordon Murray

Client:	FM Developments Ltd
Completion:	7 / 2005
Value:	10.5 M.£
Total site area:	1560m²
Apartment:	104

River Heights is a new-build residential development on the Clydeside located on a prominent site at the junction of Lancefield Quay and Hydepark Street. The development, of 104 flats, is raised on a two-storey podium of retail, commercial and car parking accommodation, creating interaction with the Clyde waterfront beyond the existing quayside building. The predominantly glazed south and east facades with internal/external balconies maximises the open aspects of the river and panoramic views of the city beyond. The glazed element of the building along with the stack bonded terracotta brick slip panels are applied in a rigorous pattern which is framed within anodised aluminium "boxes".

An external amenity space for residents is provided above the first floor car park taking advantage of the southern aspect, above the line of traffic on Lancefield Quay. Further amenity space is provided at roof level in a series of landscaped roof terraces.

The development realises an exciting and robust addition to the urban fabric of the city re-establishing links between the riverside and the city centre.

south-east view | photo Andrew Lee

ground plan 3. floor | plan Gordon Murray + Alan Dunlop

| sky terrace | photo Andrew Lee |

| penthouse | photo Andrew Lee |

RESIDENTIAL HOHENBÜHL
AGPS ARCHITECTURE

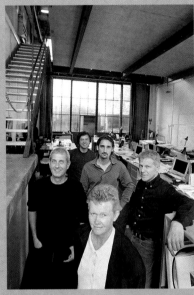
Team agps architecture

Client:	Francis T. Hodgskin
Architect:	agps architecture
	Marc Angélil, Sarah Graham,
	Manuel Scholl, Reto Pfenninger,
	Hanspeter Oester
Completion:	2004
Value:	10 M.SFr
Site area:	6150m²
Each apartment:	182m²

We are in the heart of Zurich, whose buildings, streets, parks, and plots are pocket-sized from an urban point of view. Land parcels are characteristically small, as are those reserved for residential buildings. The center piece of the project are two volumetrically discreet buildings encased by a composite skin. The two volumes enter the scene glistening in a dazzling sheath. Analogous to clothing, the sunscreen – the garment's pièce de résistance – presents itself as a coat that is both protective as well as seductively representative. What was originally used as a mass-produced mesh for conveyor belts in industrial bakeries is here transformed into a silver fabric, a curtain which acquires various complexions according to changes in light. Behind this armature, an all-glass membrane envelops the building. This is followed within by yet a further layer comprised of movable wall panels whose colors are coordinated. Silver membrane, glass, and colored plates define a triadic scene that is reinforced through constant adaptation. The three layers are flexibly interrelated and can be moved toward or away from each other. Residents choreograph their own environment. At any time of the day or year they decide on the extent of seclusion, determine what they want to see or screen. Simultaneously, they are able to define the building's appearance ranging from disguise to disclosure, from a shimmering and introverted solitude to a multitude of color combinations, or they can opt for complete transparency. Light and movement enhance the radiance of this dress. Paraphrasing Andy Warhol, Hohenbühl is "the place to think silver."

north-east view | photo Gaston Wicky

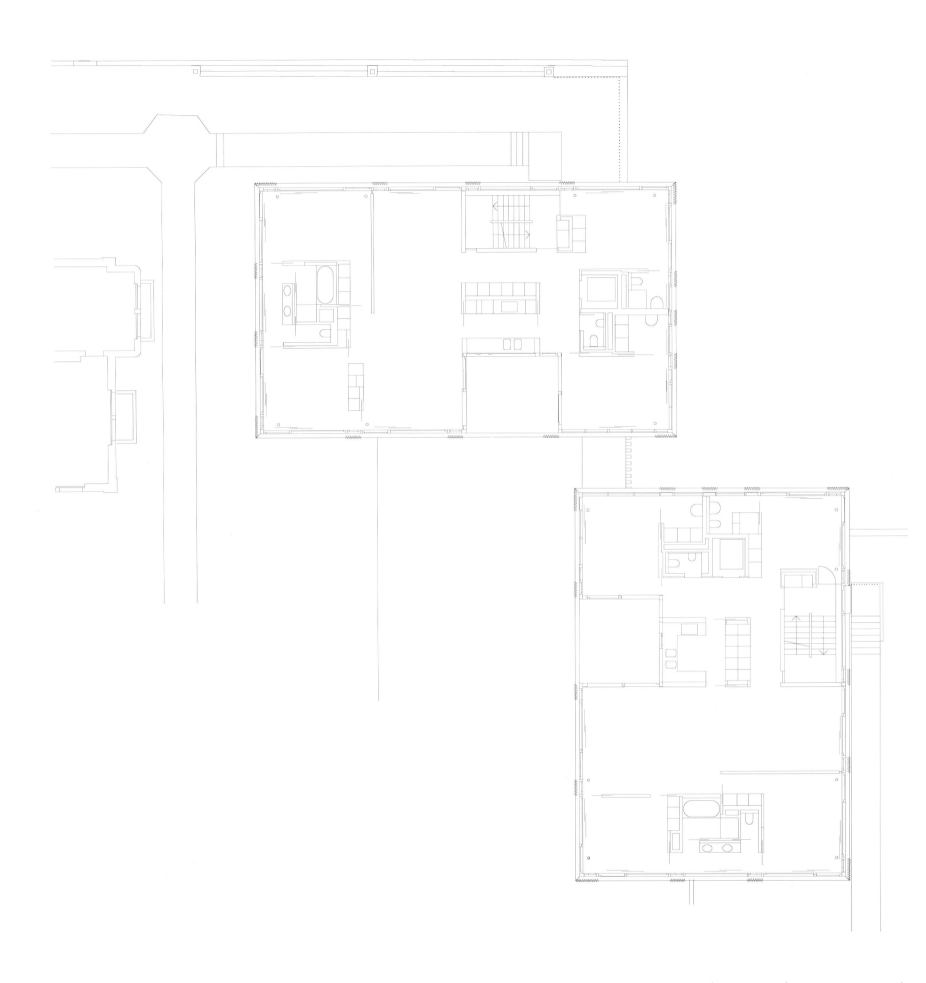

| ground plan | photo Gaston Wicky |

south elevation | photo Gaston Wicky

| apartment view | photo Gaston Wicky |

| east facade | photo Gaston Wicky

RESIDENTIAL
LIVING AT THE SUN
PETER LORENZ ATELIERS

Peter Lorenz

Client:	Tigewosi
Completion:	2005
Value:	4.2 M.€
Site area:	2530 m²
Building area:	670 m²
Floor area:	2785 m²

Austria has one of the highest standards in social housing. This corresponds to a relatively low crime rate, as well as high productivity of its citizens.

In this context, Peter Lorenz's brief is the realization of low-cost housing with flexible/attractive floorplans, generous exterior spaces/balconies, providing a specific design enabling identity and identification of the occupants.

Another important subject is the obvious requirements pertaining to ecology and sustainability (longlasting building materials, low running and maintenance costs, solar panels…)

| south elevation | photo Thomas Jantscher |

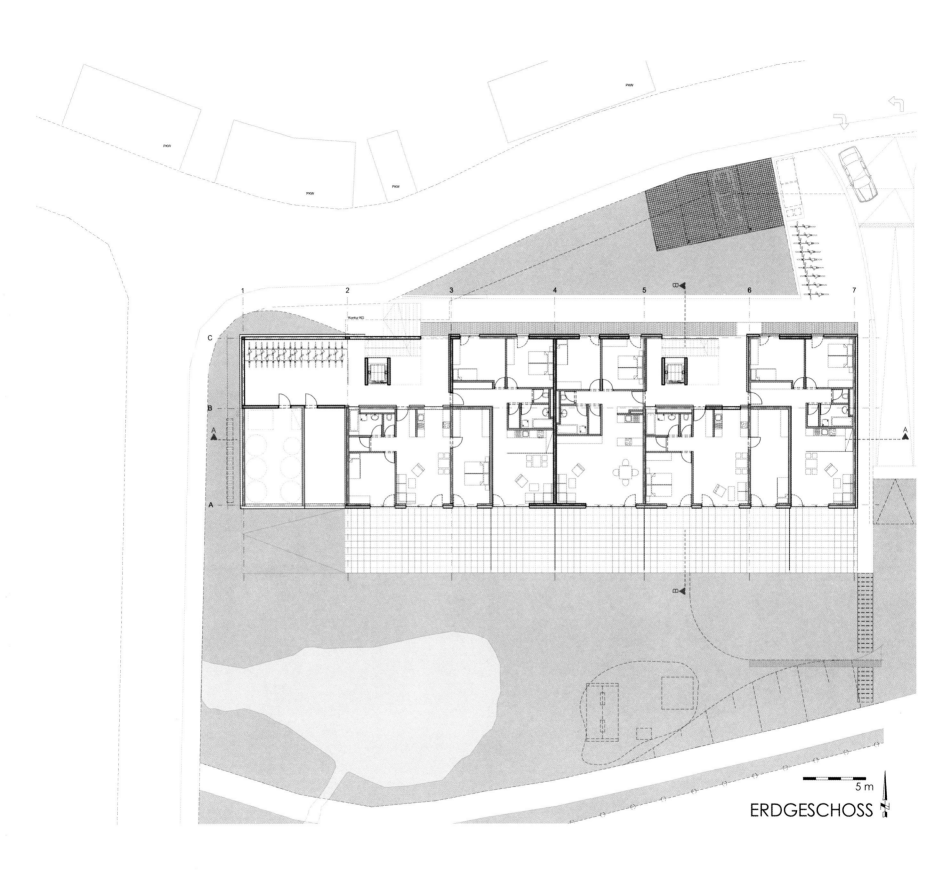

ground plan | plan Peter Lorenz Atheliers

| south-east view | photo Thomas Jantscher |

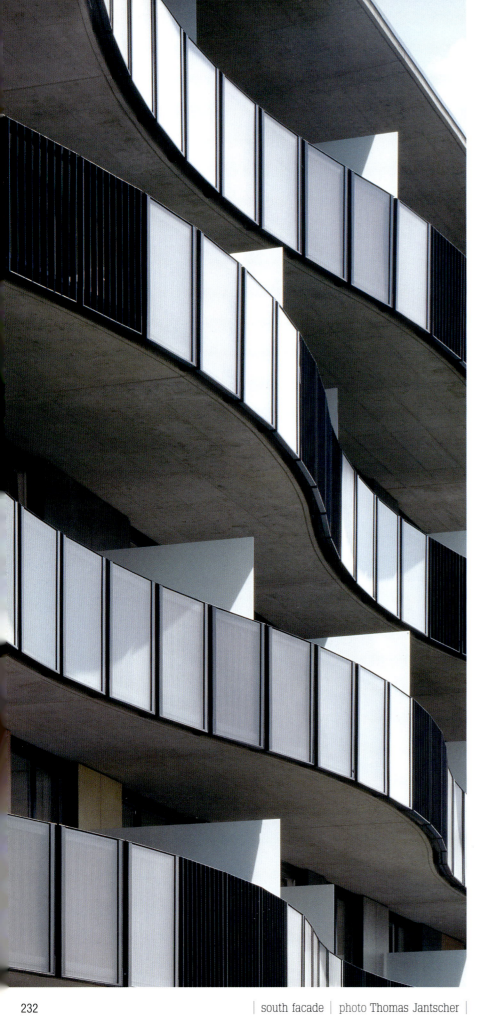

| south facade | photo Thomas Jantscher | east facade | photo Thomas Jantscher |

north-east view | photo Thomas Jantscher

RESIDENTIAL
COLONIE
BOB361 ARCHITECTS

Ivo Vanhamme   Goedele Desmet   Jean-Michel Culas

Client:	Régie Immobilière de la ville de Paris
Completion:	12 / 2003
Assistants:	Philippe De Clerck, Eveline Vyncke, Silvia De Nolf, Annelies Augustyns
Surface:	3148m² with 2604m² habitable
Budget:	3 517 500 € HT
Artist:	Yoshi Tamaki

Construction of a building with 26 apartments, 4 townhouses and 30 parking lots.

The site orientation, flanked by a park, induces the organisation of the apartments in a "strip" with a gradiant of varying openings; rather closed on the street facade to the north and widely opened on the garden side to the south, with a shifted loggia system allowing thus full illumination, and terraces for each apartment. These are orientated in the width of the building. The basic volume in grey thin bricks, is excavated to form windows, loggias, entrance hall, ... in the white "mass".

The town houses to the rear are backed to the party wall with perpendicular volumes housing the living spaces around the private patios.

| north elevation | photo Vercruysse & Dujardin |

| ground floor plan | plan BOB361 Architects |

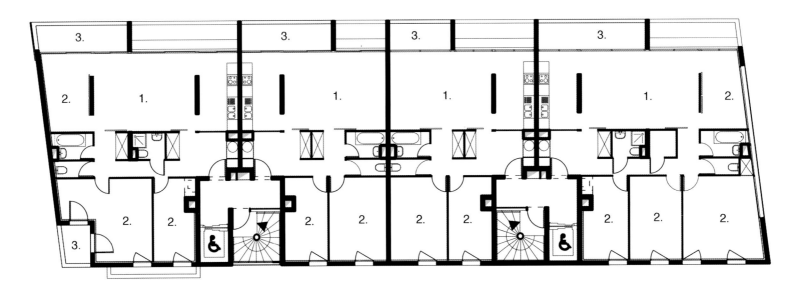

| typical floor plan | plan BOB361 Architects |

south elevation | photo Vercruysse & Dujardin

| entrance | photo Vercruysse & Dujardin |
| town houses | photo Vercruysse & Dujardin |

| north elevation | photo Vercruysse & Dujardin |

MUSEUM MERCEDES-BENZ
UNSTUDIO

Portrait: V. Bennet

Client:	DaimlerChrysler Immobilien (DCI) GmbH
Museum design:	Prof. H.G. Merz, Stuttgart
Height of the building:	47.5 m
Total area:	Approx. 53 000 m²
Floor area:	4800 m²
Exhibition area:	16 500 m²
Interior space:	210 000 m³
Levels:	9
Number of vehicles exhibited:	175

The new Mercedes-Benz Museum is located next to highway B14 at the entrance of Stuttgart. The museum covers 16 500 m² of exhibition space for the historical collection of Mercedes-Benz, which consists of 160 cars. In addition to the exhibition space, the museum houses a museum shop, a restaurant, offices and a sky lobby. Apart from the new museum building, the design also includes the development of the surrounding landscape. With 450 000 visitors a year, the existing Mercedes-Benz Museum is one of the most visited museums in Stuttgart.

The visitor proceeds through the museum from top to bottom; during the ride up the atrium in one of the three elevators, visitors are shown a multimedia Preshow presentation. The elevators are like capsules with only a large slit at eyelevel through which the visitor sees images of the history of Mercedes-Benz projected on the walls of the atrium.

south facade | photo Christian Richters

| atrium | plan Christian Richters |

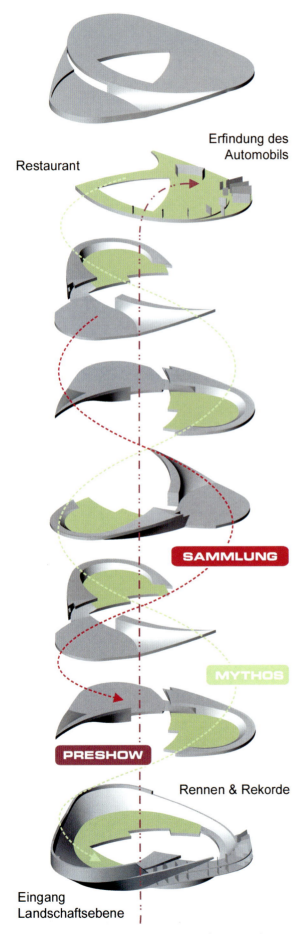

Restaurant
Erfindung des Automobils
SAMMLUNG
MYTHOS
PRESHOW
Rennen & Rekorde
Eingang Landschaftsebene

| routing | plan Unstudio |

| east view | photo Christian Richters

entrance during construction | photo Christian Richters

MUSEUM
ORDRUPGAARD MUSEUM EXTENSION
ZAHA HADID ARCHITECTS

Zaha Hadid   Portrait Steve Double

Client: Danish Ministry of Culture
Completion: 2005

The growth of the institution presents an opportunity to explore new relationships between the components of the museum and the garden that frames it, in so far that the ensemble constitutes a kind of topography in itself. The new extension seeks to establish a new landscape within the territory of its architecture, at the same time allowing new relationships with the existing conditions. The logic of the existing landscape is abstract in its geometry, new contours extend into the collection developing an alternate ground where occupancy and use are extended.

The building separates two distinct conditions of the garden and responds to them with a gradation of use that is represented by a change in transparency and access possibilities. The contour lines, which form the basis of the extension's morphology, are explored in a two-fold manner: they conform the overall enclosure, but at the same time they lay down the basis for the arrangement of the interior space. The variation on the existing topography can be read as a progression through the interior spaces, and thus a signal for transition between uses. An interior landscape presents the visitor with a layered experience where the museum's space relates to the garden.

south-east view | photo Roland Halbe

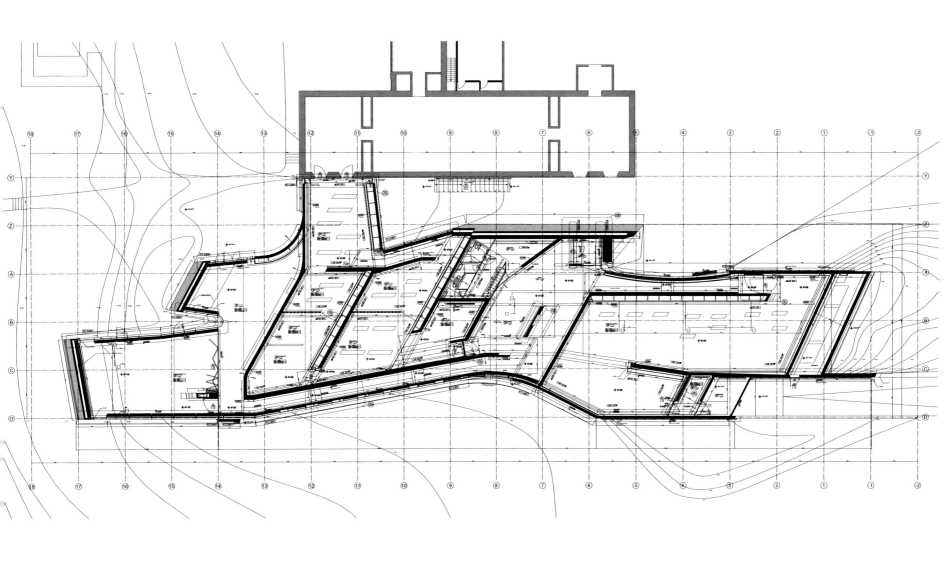

ground plan | plan Zaha Hadid Architects

west facade | photo Roland Halbe

| west elevation | photo Roland Halbe |
| corridor | photo Roland Halbe |

exhibition area | photo Roland Halbe

MUSEUM
BMW SHOWROOM
TURNER + ASSOCIATES ARCHITECTS

Client: Trivett Classic
Completion: 03 / 2006
Location: Parramatta, Sydney
Value: 4.32M.€ location
Site area: 3619m²
Building area: 3541m² including 1000m² basement carpark

The new showroom building accommodates 36 display vehicles, six delivery bays, basement and rooftop car parking and ancillary uses. An external hardstand area wrapping around the building accommodates approximately 70 vehicles.

Vehicle display, customer lounge, and sales areas occupy a vast double height volume along the length of Church Street elevated above street level. The space terminates in a ramped car display that marks the corner of the building. Capping the entire showroom, the roof cantilevers three metres past the west and south facades, providing deep overhangs.

The simplicity of the overall building form is given drama by the great volume of the space and the careful attention to the lighting that allows the cars themselves to glisten providing an ever-changing palette of colours and shapes as part of the architectural experience. Quality materials and choice furnishings and fittings make the cafe and waiting area a customer magnet in itself.

Nick Turner | Karl May | Kevin Driver | Jane Anderson

Dan Szwaj | Dom Bennett | Jon Rush | Rob Burton

| day time view from south west | photo Brett Boardman |

| view from north east | photo Brett Boardman |

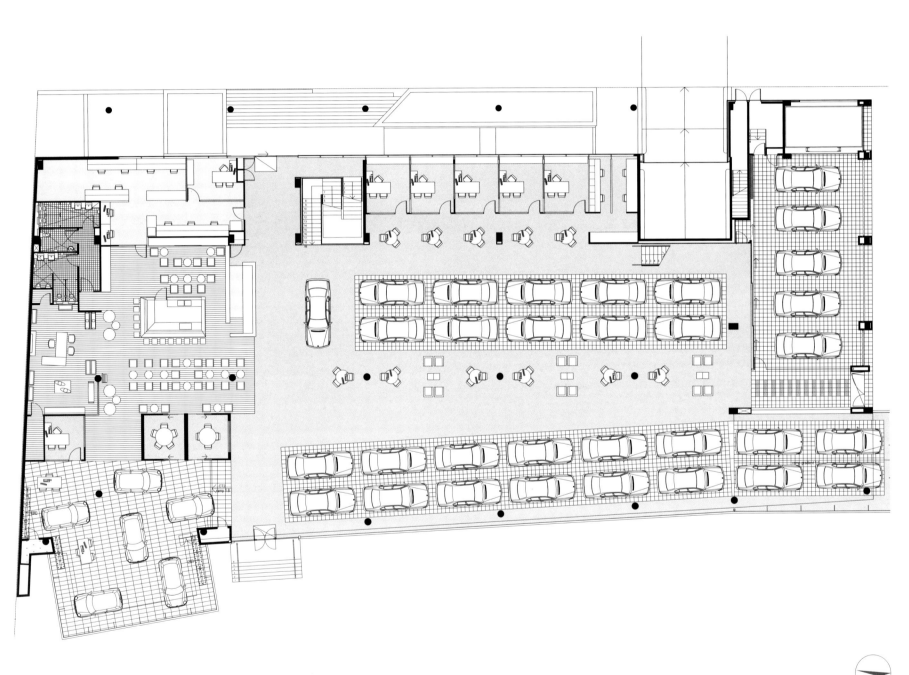

ground level plan | plan Turner + Associates Architects

| view from west on church street | photo Brett Boardman |

| Dusk view from south west | photo Brett Boardman |

| interior view | photo Brett Boardman |

| view of showroom from cafe | photo Brett Boardman |

| display box | photo Brett Boardman |

| elevated corner | photo Brett Boardman |

MUSEUM
TOUR DE MORON
MARIO BOTTA

Mario Botta   Portrait Beat Pfändler

Client: Fondation Tour de Moron, Malleray
Completion: 2004
Location: Moron a 1334 s/m, Municipality of Malleray, Jura, Switzerland
Project team: Tommaso Botta, Danilo Soldini, Guido Botta

The Moron Tower is located in the Bernese Jura on the highlands stretching from the northern edge of Switzerland towards Haute-Savoie and the Black Forest. The tower can be reached via a winding trail that snakes its way through the dense forest, starting at the village of Mallerey. The construction of this belvedere tower was inspired by the intention of giving visibility to the work done by several hundred apprentices in the region as part of their vocational training to become masons/stonecutters. After viewing the designs proposed by the apprentices, Mario Botta embraced the idea that plying a professional trade should also become a tangible sign in the landscape, and he proffered his idea of a 26-meter-tall tower with a diameter of about 6 meters. The solid stone steps are cantilevered around a hollow central bearing structure. Each step is characterised by two stone wedges embedded into vertical slabs that act as a railing. The tower is topped by a steel lookout platform that offers a 360-degree view of the surrounding countryside; to reach the belvedere, the visitor must leave the comfortable steps and climb up a narrow ladder inside the bearing cylinder. Explanatory panels around the edge of the terrace provide tourists with a description of the breathtaking panorama. A metal disc composed of two flattened cones creates a roof over the stone structure. In these mountains above the sweeping plateau, the helical tower – like an arrow driven into the terrain – comes across as an unexpected and somehow disquieting sign. Tourists and wayfarers seeking idyllic landscapes are thus drawn into the reality of austere, authentic beauty that can be found only in a place where, alongside nature, the mark of humanity is also visible.

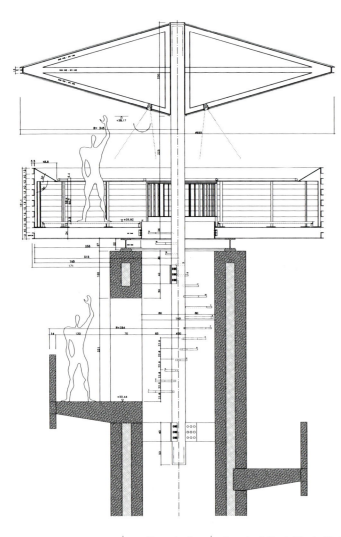

| section-studies | plan Architect Mario Botta |

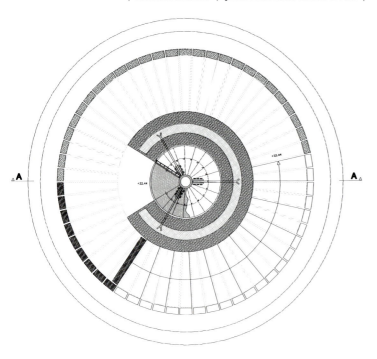

| detail-lookout platform | plan Architect Mario Botta |

| lookout platform | photo Thomas Jantscher |

tower with stair ensemble and lookout platform | photo Thomas Jantscher

INDEX GLOBAL CREATIVE ARCHITECTURE
ARCHITECT DESCRIPTION

Architects:	ABP Architekten burian+pfeiffer
	Thomas Pfeiffer Dipl.-Ing. Architekt
	Edgar Burian Dipl.-Ing. Architekt
Address:	Spicherenstrasse 6 D- 81667 München
Tel.:	0049-89-44760136
Fax:	0049-89-44760137
Email:	mail@abp-architekten.com
Web:	www.abp-architekten.com

ABP Architekten

Architects:	agps architecture
Address:	Zypressenstrasse 71 CH 8004 Zurich
Tel.:	+41 44 298 20 20
Fax:	+41 44 298 20 21
Email:	architektur@agps.ch
Web:	www.agps.ch

agps Architecture

The work of ABP Architekten focuses in housing and public buildings. Our design shows no architectural brand. With every new task we start all over again, so every building is quite different to the other.

Genius loci.
The initial situation of our architecture is always the special location, the surrounding of the building site and the question, what will be the right answer to this place. In the end of the planning process the result has to be like a custom-made suit for the place and the client.

History.
the inspiration to design a new building is based on the principle of historic architecture. We can find nearly everything done before in former times. Using this pool we find the key to create novelty in the recognition of the principals and separate them from their minor details.

Architects:	Aicher Architekten
Address:	6890 Lustenau / Vorarlberg /Austria
Tel.:	0043 5577 62654 0
Fax:	0043 5577 62654 9
Email:	office@aicher-architekten.at
Web:	www.aicher-architekten.at

Aicher Architekten

1989: diploma degree at the academy of the forming arts in Vienna.
1989 to 1997: worked in the studio prof. Wilhelm Holzbauer in Vienna. Supervising and realization as a project leader on projects in Berlin, Budapest and Austria.

Foundation of the own office 1997 in Lustenau. Since 2000 in collaboration with Arch. Karin Aicher. The office has 8 – 10 employees. The office branches in Lustenau and Innsbruck complete projects in Austria and the neighboring countries.

With a high measure of experience, flexibility and communications capacity our team completed all different planning projects. We have no special focal points in the working field of architecture and develop our design out of the situation and the relation to the place and the environment for each of the projects. With this principle, we create differentiated and individual solutions. The use of place-specific materials and resources is a central factor of our work .

Architects:	Architekturwerkstatt Dipl. Ing. Arno Bereiter
Address:	STEINEBACH 3, A-6850 DORNBIRN,
Tel.:	O5572/34229
Fax:	34245
Email:	office@arnobereiter.at

Arno Breiter

Years ago I decided to keep the staff very small. The decision includes of course, the fact that I can't do every job, so I have to say sometimes "No, I'm not able to do it properly, no capacity – so it's better for both". Some are waiting until I've got time for their project.

I still want to do nearly all the designs and detail planning by myself – the only way to get satisfied in doing architecture. If I make a mistake, it's mine and I don`t have to be angry about someone – and that's a quality in working.

I studied architecture and that's only way to be an architect – starting up with more than 4 in a team – I should have studied as a lawyer or economist.
That's my way!

Scope of work:
Concept, complete design of the buildings and also the complete interior – furniture
No construction management

Architects:	Architektur Consult ZT GmbH
Address:	Körblergasse 100, A-8010 Graz
Tel.:	+43 / 316 / 32 31 00 - 0
Fax:	+43 / 316 / 32 31 00 - 30
Email:	office@archconsult.com
Web:	www.archconsult.com

Architektur Consult ZT GmbH

Günther Domenig (born in Carinthia in 1934) is the most prominent of the so-called "Graz Architects". He studied architecture at Graz Technical University. For ten years he and Eilfried Huth were partners in an architectural business. Since 1973 he has operated his own offices in Vienna, Graz and Klagenfurt.He has won numerous awards and has had his work exhibited all over the world. His extensive oeuvre in Austria and abroad ranges from jewellery through opera stages to complex large buildings. From 1980 to 2000 he was professor at the Institute for Building Construction, Housing and Design at Graz Technical University.

Hermann Eisenköck (born in Salzburg in 1954) studied architecture at Graz Technical University. From 1981 he was office manager at Günther Domenig's office. Five years later he became managing partner at the architects' working community Domenig-Eisenköck; but he remained formally independent. Eisenköck has been awarded numerous prizes. He is a founding member and board member of Design-Stiftung Österreich, as well as board member of Stiftung Österreichischer Skulpturenpark. Since 1998, together with Herfried Peyker, he has been managing partner of Architektur Consult ZT GmbH.

Herfried Peyker (born in Carinthia in 1947) spent a year as assistant at Ljubljana Technical University following his studies at Graz Technical University. He has also worked for professor Edo Ravnikar.From 1976 to 1981 he worked at Werkgruppe Graz, and in 1982, together with Werner Nussmüller and Nikolaus Schuster, he founded the architects' office Gruppe 3. Peyker started his own office in 1995 and since then his work has focussed on urban planning, spatial development and in particular, on public buildings and social housing. This earned him many awards, especially in residential and timber construction.Since 1998, together with Hermann Eisenköck, he has been managing partner of Architektur Consult ZT GmbH.

Architects:	Architektengruppe N+M GmbH
Address:	Berliner Straße 77 63065 Offenbach Germany
Tel.:	+49 (0)69 / 8203 0
Fax:	+49 (0)69 / 8203 200
Email:	offenbach@n-plus-m.de
Web:	www.n-plus-m.de

Architektengruppe N+M

The Architektengruppe N+M GmbH is an emerging architectural office headquartered in Offenbach/Main and an office in Berlin. The business activities cover all services in architecture, interior design and urban development, building management, project development and Consulting. The experiences of the founders and the staff members are particularly in the fields of high-rises, administration buildings, projects for refurbishment, renovation and reconstruction, major hospitals and retail and entertainment centres. As service provider for the client, N+M ensures greatest possible budget security for the client by the continuous examination of architecture, technical feasibility, functional connections as well as economic aspects (costing and date monitoring). An internal project management provides a smooth flow of project process. A scheduled, technical-coordinated and economic project process is guaranteed by clearly defined responsibilities within the project-team, configuration of a project-related communication- and data-management and formulation of an obligatory project-manual

Architects:	Architectenbureau Paul de Ruiter bv
Address:	Leidsestraat 8-10 NL-1017 PA Amsterdam
Tel.:	+31 (0)20 - 626 32 44
Fax:	+31 (0)20 - 623 70 02
Email:	info@paulderuiter.nl
Web:	www.paulderuiter.nl

Architectenbureau Paul de Ruiter bv

Research and experiments can lead to buildings and cities in which people feel comfortable without jeopardizing the environment and the economic feasibility. This, in a nutshell, is the philosophy of Architectenbureau Paul de Ruiter which was founded in 1994 in Amsterdam, the Netherlands.

The aim is to create synergy by integrating architecture with the construction and its installations, and the application of new technologies and scientific research. This can only be done by intense cooperation and the sharing of knowledge of all parties involved. Only then an impulse can be given to the modernisation of architecture and urban design. Only then is it possible to exceed the expectations of the users, the commissioner and its environment.

The commissions handled by Architectenbureau Paul de Ruiter range from urban design studies, industrial buildings, housing to interior designs and industrial design. The office is staffed by enthusiasts whose distinctive feature is that they all believe in the power of discovery.

Architects:	Atelier 5 Architekten und Planer AG
Address:	Sandrainstrasse 3, CH-3001 Bern
Tel.:	+41 (0)31 327 52 52
Fax:	+41 (0)31 327 52 50
Email:	atelier5@atelier5.ch
Web:	www.atelier5.ch

Atelier 5 Architekten und Planer AG

Atelier 5 is located in Bern, the capital of Switzerland. This year it celebrates its 50th birthday. The founding of Atelier 5 is closely linked with housing design, specifically with the Halen housing scheme. Nevertheless there is no specialisation in a single design field as far as the office is concerned. However one could say, that "living" stands in the foreground, since the well being of the user is always considered an essential issue. This is true in the conception of all projects, irrespective of whether they regard, schools, hospitals, industrial or administrative buildings. Those tasks, together with the schemes in the areas of town planning and urban design, constitute the base of the Atelier 5 work.

Atelier 5 is operative throughout Europe. Its long-term teamwork experience qualifies it for interdisciplinary projects, be it as leaders or as participants in a project team. In the last ten years Atelier5 won various international competitions. The resulting buildings can be visited in Hamburg (the Rotherbaum housing estate), in Mainz (the Dreikönigshöfe housing estate) and in Potsdam (the judiciary centre of Brandenburg).

Architects:	Auer+Weber+Assoziierte GmbH	
Address:	Haussmannstrasse 103A	Georgenstrasse 22
	D-70188 Stuttgart	D-80799 Munich
Tel.:	+49 (0)711 268 404 0	+49 (0)89 381 617 0
Fax:	+49 (0)711 268 404 88	+49 (0)89 381 617 38
Email:	stuttgart@auer-weber.de	muenchen@auer-weber.de
Web:	www.auer-weber.de	

Auer+Weber+Assoziierte GmbH

The architectural office Auer+Weber+Assoziierte originates from the Auer+Weber architectural group existing since 1980. With offices in Munich and Stuttgart, the company employs an average of between 50 and 60 personnel.

The focal point of activities is the conception and design of new buildings and alterations for public-sector institutions and private clients, increasingly as total service planning consultants or in collaboration with investors and construction companies. Over the past few years, we have been increasingly involved in the design and realisation of international projects.

The common characteristic of all projects lies in the distinctive and coherent development of architecture which emerges from the specific brief and unique site conditions.

Design activities range from projects for education and research, administration and culture, hotels and residential buildings as well as sports facilities and transportation buildings, to urban development and master plans.

Architects:	BOB361 architectes
Address:	Rue Lambert Crickx 16 1070 Brussels
Tel.:	0032/2 511 07 91
Fax:	0032/2 511 86 07
Email:	bxl@bob361.com

BOB361 architects

BOB361's thorough examination of an assignment does not aim at continuously reinventing the discipline of architecture, but at getting rid of ballast and white noise, and at bringing in the right expertise so as to make room for making architecture. Irrespective of the sort of assignment, and the assumptions inherent in the situations or programmes at hand, bob361 applies the same professionalism, not only when analyzing and researching the data that come with the assignment, but also and primarily when developing the specific solution, all the way through the design process up to the fine details.

By adopting an attitude that focuses on the assignment and what is has to offer, bob361 does distance itself from intentions or agendas that do not contribute to a solution. Probably because the architects reject such ballast, the work or oeuvre of bob361 is able to create its own environment.

In circumstances that sometimes consist of only white noise, as conglomerates of different requirements, demands or insights rather then well-designed and thought out situations, the projects affirm themselves as no-nonsense responses to questions that have never before been asked.

Architects:	Burckhardt+Partner AG
Address:	Dornacherstrasse 210 CH 4002 Basel
Tel.:	+41 61 338 34 34
Fax:	+41 61 338 34 35
Email:	basel@burckhardtpartner.ch
Web:	www.burckhardtpartner.ch

Burckhardt+Partner AG

Burckhardt+Partner AG is one of Switzerland's leading architectural and general planning practices. Providing high quality service is the central objective of our work. Working closely with the client we identify his needs, define project goals and thus develop and implement optimized design solutions, taking all relevant factors into account. We provide a comprehensive range of services from inception to completion, covering all aspects of construction planning from strategic planning to restoration. These are supplemented by additional services such as project management, profitability calculations, establishing contacts with investors as well as all necessary specialist services.

Burckhardt+Partner AG is active in all the major fields of construction planning. These include: Education/culture; chemistry/laboratories/pharmaceuticals; leisure/sports; health care; trade/shopping facilities; industry/commercial buildings; urban development/traffic infrastructure; tourism/hotels and catering; administration; housing.

Burckhardt+Partner AG is a stock corporation with shares held by about 40 members of the management staff.

The headquarter is situated in Basel, other offices are in Berne, Zurich, Lausanne and Geneva.

Architects:	Camenzind Evolution
Address:	Samariterstrasse 5 CH-8032 Zurich, Switzerland
Tel.:	+41 44 253 9500
Fax:	+41 44 253 9510
Email:	info@camenzindevolution.com
Web:	www.camenzindevolution.com

Camenzind Evolution

Winner of the Young Architect of the Year Award and the International Design Award, Swiss architect Stefan Camenzind has placed himself firmly within the new generation of up-and-coming architects. Fundamental to his very diverse work in progress is the fusion of design ingenuity with Swiss quality. Having gained many years of international experience in the architectural offices of Nicholas Grimshaw in London and Renzo Piano in Paris, Stefan Camenzind founded the architectural studio Camenzind Evolution in 1996, which has grown to 10-15 architects today. Many of the projects have been the result of winning architectural competition and have, like the Sports Centre Buchholz and the Seewurfel Development, won multiple awards including the Swiss Prix Fédéraux des Beaux-Arts, the German Bauwelt Award and the Royal Institute of British Architects World Wide Award.

Architects:	Eike Becker_Architects
Address:	Kochstraße 22 10969 Berlin Germany
Tel.:	+49 30 - 25 93 74 - 0
Fax:	+49 30 - 25 93 74 – 11
Email:	info@eb-a.de
Web:	www.eb-a.de

Eike Becker_Architects

Eike Becker_Architects is one of the successful young architectural practices in Germany. Numerous distinctions, awards and exhibitions document this. In 2001 Eike Becker was awarded the internationally prestigious RIBA Award and in 1998 the (German architectural) Deubau Prize. Today they work for well-known clients in Berlin, Munich, Düsseldorf, Cologne, Stuttgart, Brussels, London and New York.

In 1991 Eike Becker, Swantje and Oliver Kühn and Georg Gewers founded the partnership of Becker Gewers Kühn & Kühn Architects. Until 1994 the office was located in the former Grand Hotel Esplanade on Potsdamer Platz, then still a wasteland. Since December 1999 Eike Becker has been managing the office Eike Becker_Architects, partnered by Helge Schmidt, in the GSW skyscraper near the former Allied bordercrossing between West and East Berlin, 'Checkpoint Charlie'.

On their desks you find very different buildings and projects, such as urban projects for China, Munich and Neuss, skyscrapers for Berlin, Kiel and Chongqing; administration buildings for Prague, Düsseldorf, Berlin, Stuttgart and Hamburg, hotels for Berlin and Kiel, the representation of Boeing in Berlin and furniture designs for several manufacturers.

Though varying in scale, all their buildings and products combine high-end design with innovative engineering feats, technical precision and social responsibility.

Architects:	Shuhei Endo Architect Institute
Address:	6F,3-21,Suehiro-cho, Kita-ku, Osaka, 530-0053,Japan
Tel.:	+81-6-6312-7455
Fax:	+81-6-6312-7456
Email:	endo@paramodern.com
Web:	www.paramodern.com

Shuhei Endo

A sense of distance is receding in our lives. The world is becoming more homogeneous in a variety of ways, diminishing the environment around us. The modern architecture of the past century yielded many achievements and suggested diverse possibilities, but also turned out to be a factor promoting this homogeneity. It seems that in the end economics dominates and sets the direction for the quality of architecture. It is probably inevitable that homogeneity should prevail through technology and materials. Nevertheless, the expressive character of architecture should still not be so rigidly constrained by economic efficiency or technological factors. I admit that there exists a certain mood that sets the direction of our time, but I prefer to start with a sense of things that seems real.

This sense is that we feel physically familiar and comfortable with a state of continuity in which there are no clear boundaries between inside and outside. We experience this when enclosing a space, or wrapping our bodies with something. I feel certain that I can trust this as my starting point. I believe that a reexamination of the possibilities and validity that modern architecture once possessed, extending from this sense, can guide us in the search for a "paramodern" architecture. Pramodern here means clues to another modernism. Although it seems as if modern architecture has already been exhausted, I believe there are still are possibilities waiting to be found.

As an example, I have experimented with what we call "halftecture" that arises from open space, questioning the usual architectural objective of dissociating interior and exterior. Another example is "rooftecture", which is a method to create architectural space with a "continuous band of roof/wall" as a single element. Both of these are attempts to create non-rejective and continuous spaces, or architecture which possesses diversity even while following the rules of geometry.

Architects:	Edward Suzuki Associates Inc.
Address:	Maison Marian 3F, 15-23, 1-chome Seta, Setagaya-ku, Tokyo 158-0095
Tel.:	+81-3-3707-5272
Fax:	+81-3-3707-5274
Email:	esa@edward.net
Web:	www.edward.net

EDWARD SUZUKI ASSOCIATES INC.

Edward Suzuki was born in Saitama, Japan, in 1947 of Japanese and German parentage. He attended Notre Dame University to earn his B. of Arch, and later attended Harvard University to earn his M. of Arch in Urban Design. He worked for Buckminster Fuller and Sadao while at Harvard, and then went on to work for Kenzo Tange & URTEC in Tokyo. He established his own practice in1977 and with a staff of seven to ten, depending on the number of part-timers, works on various kinds of projects ranging from private houses to commercial, institutional, and transportation facilities. Of late, his office has designed the first case of an industrialized house in Japan (and perhaps in the world) designed by an architect and built by a major housing manufacturer, Daiwa House Kougyo, in a collaborative effort. "EDDI's House"is named after the architect's nickname and also stands for Edward Daiwa-House Design Innovation.

Architects:	FRüH ARCHITEKTUR büro ZT Gmbit
Address:	Lochbachstraße 6 A - 6971 Hard
Tel.:	+43 (0) 5574 - 77 44 7 -12
Fax:	+43 (0) 5574 - 77 44 7 -10
Email:	office@frueh.at
Web:	www.frueh.at

FRüH ARCHITEKTUR büro ZT Gmbit

We base our work on user requirements, functional and financial conditions, secret and unusual wishes. Before the planning stage, we analyze each and every justification down to the last detail and develop the idea to the best of our ability. Based on the premise that scarcely any manmade construction other than buildings makes us conscious of, and enables us to experience the three-dimensional space around us, we strive to create a strong spatial awareness in the residents and users of our buildings, which makes orientation easier and facilitates incorporation in larger structures.

Fields of activity:
Architecture, interior design, furniture design

Building typology:
Industrial/commercial buildings, residential buildings/detached houses, interior design, design of individual items of furniture www.circumflex.at

Architects:	Gerber Architekten
Address:	Tönnishof 9, 44149 Dortmund
Tel.:	+49/231/9065–0
Fax:	+49/231/9065–111
Email:	kontakt@gerberarchitekten.de
Web:	www.gerberarchitekten.de

Gerber Architekten

For more than three decades Eckhard Gerber has created a constantly growing and rich portfolio of architectural work at home and abroad. Gerber and his staff see architecture as a service which achieves all-round success through intensive and productive cooperation with all of their project partners, clients and users. This leads to designs which are individual solutions, but which collectively form a consistent work of enduring buildings and show the virtues of an architecture that is clear and functional in the best sense.

The architectural forms which Eckhard Gerber uses in his designs are obviously indebted to classical Modernism. They recognise the quality of clear geometry as a rational and yet artistic design feature, both independently and in a more differentiated and complex composition. The details fit into the whole; the functional and social inner structure is revealed by the outside appearance and merges with the surrounding environment. At the same time, this contrasts fundamentally with trends in modern architecture to negate the local settings: Gerber's buildings form part of the situation into which they are placed and from which they develop.

Architects:	Giovanni Vaccarini Architetto
Address:	Corso Garibaldi n. No. 24 64021 Giulianova, Teramo, Italy
Tel.:	+39 085 8028625 / 329 8626587
Email:	giovannivaccarini@tin.it
Web:	www.giovannivaccarini.it

Giovanni Vaccarini

Giovanni Vaccarini was born in Orta Nova (FG) on November 19, 1966.He graduated in 1993 with full marks in Architecture at the University of Studies "G. D'Annunzio" in Pescara.In 1994 he won a prize for a specialisation about landscape architecture at the Waterloo University, Environmental Studies, School of Architecture Ontario - Canada.He is research doctor (PhD) - architectural composition.

From 1995 to 2001 he has been teaching and carrying out research at the Faculty of Architecture at the University "G. D'Annunzio" in Pescara.Currently he is Visiting Professor.

Founder of the Aid'A, the Italian Agency of Architecture and he practises the profession of architect in his own firm He works with the ambitious to measure himself with the practise of making things and the idea to affirm his projects like a collective experience.

Architects:	Gordon Murray and Alan Dunlop architects
Address:	Breckenridge House 274
	Sauchiehall Street Glasgow.
Tel.:	0141-331-2926
Fax:	0141-332-6790
Email:	mail@murraydunloparchitects.com
Web:	www.murraydunloparchitects.com

Gordon Murray + Alan Dunlop

On 1st June 1999 the Practice of Glass Murray Architects became Gordon Murray + Alan Dunlop Architects to reflect the strength of the partnership and the progressive nature of the Practice which was established in 1931. In addition to the two Partners, the Practice has six senior managers – Project Directors – and a Practice Secretary. This team is responsible for the day-to-day running of the Practice and its projects. They are backed up by a team of 25 or so architects, technicians and assistants to deliver these projects.

Over the years the Practice has gained a reputation for service, quality of design and integrity of purpose. These attributes still form the basis of the firm's philosophy. The work of the Practice has however expanded to cover all aspects of the built environment. In addition to new build work, our firm is committed to a programme of conservation, sensitive urban renewal and regeneration initiatives.

Our core function is design and delivery of architecture in its widest sense. In support of that skill we have developed specific areas of specialism in the built environment and construction: urban design, Master Planning, urban landscaping, conservation, project management and planning supervision.

Architects:	Hilmer & Sattler und Albrecht Gesellschaft von Architekten mbH
Address:	Sophienstr. 33A, 10178 Berlin
Tel.:	030 / 284 954 -20
Fax:	030 / 280 71 33
Email:	info@h-s-a.de
Web:	www.h-s-a.de

Hilmer & Sattler u. Albrecht

The office Hilmer & Sattler became established 1974 by Heinz Hilmer and Christoph Sattler in Munich, the branch in Berlin exists since 1988. Thomas Albrecht joined the office in 1986, since 1997 is the office known under the name Hilmer & Sattler and Albrecht GmbH.

The planning focal points lie in the high-value dwelling building and office building, as well as in the museum and hotel building. Cities structural projects are a further essential component of the work field. Next to new construction projects, also reconstruction and restorations belong to the achievement spectrum which is offered to public and private builders.

Altogether 35 colleagues, who are qualified without exception as diploma engineers and architects, as well as two secretaries comprises the average office strength.

The office Hilmer & Sattler and Albrecht is active nationwide and offers the complete preinvestment phase 1-9.

Architects:	J. MAYER H.
Address:	Bleibtreustr. 54 D-10623 Berlin Germany
Tel.:	+49 30 31 50 61 17
Fax:	+49 30 31 50 61 18
Email:	contact@jmayerh.de
Web:	www.jmayerh.de

J. MAYER H.

J.MAYER H. Architects have been working on the interface between product design, architecture, urban planning and communication for more than 8 years. Projects are developed and supervised from the concept to the realization. In this process, a strong emphasis has been placed on the networking of various competent partners from different disciplines. Specific research projects, developed in collaboration with international Universities, are considered another important aspect in the work of the office.

Architects:	Architect Mario Botta
Address:	Via Ciani 16 CH-6904 Lugano, Switzerland
Tel.:	0041 91 972 86 25
Fax:	0041 91 970 14 54
Email:	info@botta.ch
Web:	www.botta.ch

Mario Botta

Botta was born in Mendrisio, Ticino on April 1, 1943. After an apprenticeship with the architectural firm of Carloni and Camenisch in Lugano, Botta first attended the Art College in Milan and then studied at the University Institute of Architecture in Venice. Directed by Carlo Scarpa and Giuseppe Mazzariol, he received his professional degree in 1969. During his time in Venice, he had the opportunity to meet and work for Le Corbusier and Louis I. Kahn. His professional activity began in 1970 in Lugano. He built his first single-family house in Canton Ticino, and subsequently all over the world.

He has always committed himself to architectural research. Since 1996, he has been involved as creator and founder of a new academy of architecture in Ticino. His work has achieved international renown, important awards and has been presented at many exhibitions.

His notable realizations include SFMOMA in San Francisco, the cathedral in Evry, the Museum Jean Tinguely in Basel, the Cymbalista synagogue and Jewish Heritage Centre in Tel Aviv, the MART museum of modern and contemporary art in Rovereto, Kyobo Tower in Seoul, the office building Tata CS in New Delhi and Hyderabad, the church and pastoral centre Pope John XXIII in Seriate, and the restoration of the Theatre alla Scala in Milan.

Architects:	Mecanoo Architecten B.v.
Address:	Oude Delft 203 2611 HD Delft
Tel.:	+31 (0)15-279 8100
Fax:	+31 (0)15-279 8111
Email:	info@mecanoo.nl
Web:	www.mecanoo.nl

Mecanoo Architecten

Mecanoo has produced several outstanding projects during its 25 years of existence. Architect / director Francine Houben (1955) is opposed to too stringent interpretations of her professional area. For her, architecture is not only designing a building. The area of her attention is much wider: "Architecture is a combination of various elements, like town and landscape planning and interior design. Mecanoo's work is characterised by the integration of these disciplines".

In Mecanoo's designs, technical, human and playful aspects are interwoven into one solution. Houben: "Architecture should touch the senses. Architecture can never be a purely intellectual, conceptual and visual game. What counts in the end is the interweaving of form and emotion."

The practice is very successful in the Netherlands and Europe. The concern for the expressive potential of space, form and material is combined with a reflective practice on the dialogue with clients and future users. Because of this multi-disciplinary approach, the projects of Mecanoo's receive a great deal of attention. This finds expression in the various prizes the firm has garnered, among which are the Maaskant prize for young architects 1987, the Jhr. Victor de Stuers medal 1994 for Herdenkingsplein in Maastricht, the National Steel Award 1998 and the Corus Construction Award 2000 for the Delft University of Technology, the Building Quality Award 2000 for housing project Nieuw Terbregge in Rotterdam, the A.M. Schreuders Prize 2001 for the office villa Maliebaan 16 in Utrecht and the TECU Architecture Award 2001 and the Dutch Building Prize 2003 for the National Heritage Museum in Arnhem.

Architects:	Muramatsu Architects
Address:	4-8-18-504 Kitasinjuku Shinjuku-ku, Tokyo, 169-0074 Japan
Tel.:	+81-3-3362-1915
Fax:	+81-3-3362-1921
Email:	m-arch@netlaputa.ne.jp
Web:	www.japan-architects.com/muramatsu-architects

Muramatsu Motoyasu

Motoyasu Muramatsu founded Muramatsu Architects as a design-oriented office in Tokyo in 1993. Motoyasu Muramatsu has worked on a variety of public and private works. He has extensive experience in the care facilities for the elderly, residential work and furniture design. Other projects include medical facilities, church, commercial facilities, pachinko-parlors, offices, museum, educational facility, and aquarium. He establishes a beautiful presence in the environment, and evokes a feeling of balmy atmosphere, whether in city, suburb or countryside.

His theme is to penetrate into the relationship between people and environments, to convert those invisible relationships into tangible forms.

His objective is to create architectural serial spaces, places and times that establish relationships between people and environments where people live, in order to enable people to experience those spaces and times to liberate themselves from many pre–conceptions and stresses of contemporary society and to rediscover themselves and to believe in being happy.

Architects:	Karim and Rames Najjar
Address:	Seidlgasse 41 / 5a A-1030 Vienna Austria
Tel :	+43(0)1 -595 34 08
Fax :	+43(0)1 -595 34 08-60
Email:	office@najjar-najjar.com
Web:	www.najjar-najjar.com

Najjar & Najjar

Najjar & Najjar Architects is a studio for architecture, planning and design led by the brothers Karim and Rames Najjar. Their studio was established in Vienna, Austria, in 1999. Since then it was making its name with highly original work. The designs are not only architecturally innovative and visually striking, but are also pieces of highly functional equipment - inspired by both nature and technologies transferred from other industries.

The scope of its work includes design of buildings, bridges, exhibitions and yachts. The practice is recognised for consistently challenging traditional pre-conceptions of space and demonstrating environmental concern and efficiency, without the need to compromise on contemporary form. Research is a vital ingredient for the practice and a balance between experimental and real projects is kept in order to remain at the cutting-edge of the field.

Architects:	O.F.D.A.
Address:	Arakicho-14, Shinjuku-ku, Tokyo, Japan
Tel.:	+81-3-3358-4303
Fax:	+81-3-3358-4304
Web:	www.ofda.jp

O.F.D.A.

O.F.D.A. a shortened form for "Office For Diverse Architects". The office was founded in 1998 by Taku Sakaushi and Hiroyuki Ito, who had been formerly working for the largest architectural design firm "nikken sekkei". Now the office consists of each three architects' office with the joining of Chika Kijima in 1999 and about 10 staff work together.

The office has designed many houses, complex housings and other social facilities(factories ,educational facilities and so on) . Many works have been featured in books and magazines and given prizes.

The re-tem factory, designed by Taku Sakaushi and assistant architect Takeshi Nakashima, was firstly shown in Japan's most major architecture magazine "shin-kenchiku" and won the prize of "Ashihara-Yoshinobu Award" ,which is positioned as the new-face award of the organization "AACA"(Japan Association Of Artists Craftsman & Architects).

Architects:	Peter W. Schmidt Architekt BDA	
Address:	Kuppenheimstraße 4 75179 Pforzheim	Lützowstraße 102-104 10785 Berlin
Tel.:	+49 7231-4539-0	+49 30-230 861-0
Fax:	+49 7231-4539-90	+49 30-230 861-90
Email:	pforzheim@pws.eu	berlin@pws.eu
Web:	www.pws.eu	

Peter W. Schmidt Architekten

The architectural office Peter W. Schmidt, situated in Berlin and Pforzheim, has worked for 15 years towards a integral approach towards architecture. By looking at the realized projects, the office's versatility becomes apparent: Besides prominent villas and apartment buildings, the team realized large-scale projects such as hospitals, office-buildings, industrial buildings and cultural centres. Design, architectonical expression and functionality of Peter W. Schmidt's buildings received numerous awards.

The office focuses especially on the analysis of the building's context and the collaboration with the client. Peter W. Schmidt doesn't construe architecture as a fashionable add-on to required functions, rather than as a complex relationship between space and timeless ideals. By expressing a strong architectonical concept, the building's form becomes legible as well as the details mirror the underlying design principles. The office of Peter W. Schmidt stands for the highest quality in planning and execution of architectural projects.

Architects:	project A.01 architects ZT GmbH
Address:	mariahilfer straße 101/3/48, 1060 vienna, austria
Tel.:	+43 1 5268826
Fax:	+43 1 526 99 91
Email:	office@schmitzer.com
Web:	www.schmitzer.com

Project A01 Architects (Schmitzer)

The architectural division project A.01 architects ZT GmbH, founded 2005, focuses on the design and realisation of buildings and furniture as well as lighting and graphic design. Unique and sometimes experimental building skins are developed for each project.

The interior design division, existing since 1997, creates environments for future-oriented firms and individuals. New spaces for living and working have been developed over the years, always questioning the traditional functionalities and forms.

Pm1 is the project management division, it concentrates on the realisation of projects and the building process. The development of tools like webcost, a controlling application, is also an integral part of this department.

Architects:	Peter Lorenz	
Address:	A-6020 Innsbruck Maria-Theresien-Str. 37	A-1010 Wien Franz-Josefs-Kai 45
Tel.:	0043/ (0)512/ 58 68 45	0043/ (0)1/ 532 81 84
Fax:	0043/ (0)512/56 18 93	0043/ (0)1/ 532 81 11
Email:	office@peterlorenz.at	
Web:	www.peterlorenz.at	

Peter Lorenz

philosophy
Our teamwork is based on creativity, efficiency and spontaneous flexibility. We consider the positive atmosphere in our team and with our partners as the most important element for the highly successful organisation of our work.

services
ARCHITECTURAL SERVICES do include feasibility studies, architectural design, detailed planning, general planninig,site supervision, project management, 3D modelling, sustainability concept DESIGN interior design, furniture design,guidance systems, corporated and graphic design,holistic appearance design, URBAN PLANNING project development, urban masterplans, layout plan, CATCHMENT AREA (so far) Austria, Northern Italy, Slovenia, Hongkong, China.

organisation
The office has developed and established an "office standard" since 2002 on the basis of internal experiences and external consultancy. This standard controls and directs each activity in the office. As a team we strongly believe in flat hierarchies. Nevertheless the responsibility for each project is allocated to the project managers. For quality control we have established an efficient system to ensure optimal output. The project manager has one staff member allocated to his project as an outside controller – one person with a fresh and unbiased look and opinion regarding the design.

location
main office in Innbruck since 1980.
branch in Vienna since 1991 – for all other destinations we work with our local and international partners.

Architects:	Pichler & Traupmann Architects
Address:	Kundmanngasse 39/12 1030 Vienna Austria
Tel.:	0043-1-7133203
Email:	office@pxt.at
Web:	www.pxt.at

Pichler & Traupmann Architects

Christoph Pichler
born	1964 in Vienna
education	University of Applied Arts in Vienna (1983 – 89)
	Harvard University Graduate School of Design (1990 – 92)
teaching	since 1992 Vienna Technical University
	since 2003 Graz Technical University
	Guest Critic, Harvard University Graduate School of Design (2006)
studio	since 1992 Pichler & Traupmann in Vienna

Johann Traupmann
born	1958 in Güssing/Burgenland
education	Theology at Vienna University (1977 – 83)
	Architecture at the University of Applied Arts in Vienna (1981 – 87)
teaching	since 1992 University of Applied Arts in Vienna
	since 2002 Assistant Professor at the University of Applied Arts in Vienna
studio	since 1992 Pichler & Traupmann in Vienna

Pichler & Traupmann, Architects
1997	Prize for Architecture of the Austrian Cement Industry
1998	Prize of the Austrian Architects' Association
2002	Prize for Architecture to the Federal State of Burgenland
2003	Contribution to the Latent Utopias Show in Graz
2004	Honorable Mention for ADIDAS Brand Center, International Competition
2006	Prize for Architecture of the Federal State of Burgenland

Architects:	Querkraft Architekten ZT GmbH
Address:	Dunkl - Erhartt - Sapp Austria 1060 Vienna mariahilferstrasse 51
Tel.:	+43-1-548 77 11
Fax:	+43-1-548 77 11-44
Email:	office@querkraft.at
Web:	www.querkraft.at

querkraft architekten ZT GmbH

Since 2000 Querkiaft has participated at exhibitions in the USA, Slovakia, Slovenia, Hungary, Czech Republic, Brazil, Japan and China, with various publications in magazines like „architektur aktuell", „ bauform", „architektur", „wettbewerbe", „bauwelt", „detail" and „ga-houses". In 2001 guest-professorsship at the Roger Williams University in Rhode Island, USA. In 2002 awarded the " Austrian Prize for Costumers of Architecture" for the industrial building of „trevision". Beside social housing, more and more architectural projects to buildings for offices, trade, commerce and industry. 2004 Austrian contribution to 9. la biennale di Venezia. 2004 prize of the city of Vienna for architecture. 2004 young architect of the year award. Since 2006, professorship Akademie der Bildenden künste München (per sapp). 2006 award for good buildings in France/Germany for adidas brand center in Herzogenaurach/Germany. Also in 2006 award "built 2005". 2006 Querkraft won the competition for building the "Museum Collection Liaunig" in Carinthia/Austria.

We work in a team. The art of lateral thinking starts our creative strategies. Personal diversities open the horizons of our team. The human being forms the center of our work. Architecture's meaning is also its use. Planning is a process, the client a partner. Architecture is art. Good architecture is sustainable, appropriate and physical. Its beauty comes from the inside. The content shapes the building.

Architects:	Ricardo Bofill Taller De Arquitectura
Address:	Avda. Industria, 14-08960 Sant Just Desvern-Barcelone
Tel.:	34-93 499 99 00
Fax:	34-93 499 99 50
Email:	tallerbcn@bofill.com
Web:	www.bofill.com

Ricardo Bofill

Ricardo Bofill was born in Barcelona. In 1963 he founded the Taller de Arquitectura (Architectural Workshop), an international team with headquarters in Barcelona, which takes on projects of city planning, transport, leisure, housing and offices.

City design has been applied in the European cities of Luxembourg, Rome, Prague, Warsaw and Madrid, as well as in Boston, USA. In China, the team is constructing a hotel and two housing complexes. Concerning great Spanish infrastructures, Barcelona Airport extension will be completed in 2008 and the Valladolid Auditorium is under construction.

Housing is another area intensely studied by Taller de Arquitectura, especially the great social residential complex carried out in the Paris region as well in Barcelona, Stockholm, the Hague and Beijing.

Several office buildings have also been realized: the most relevant examples are the offices for Bank Paribas, Cartier, Dior, Axa Insurances in Paris, Corso Karlin in Prague, Atrium Saldanha in Lisbon, the office towers, 'Shiseido Building' in Tokyo, 'Dearborn Center', and 'Donnelley Building', both in Chicago.

Architects:	suppose design office
Address:	13-2-3F kako-machi naka-ku hiroshima JPN
Tel./Fax:	+81-82-247-1152
Email:	info@suppose.jp
Web:	www.suppose.jp

Suppose Design Office

Suppose Design Office is an architectural design office based in Hiroshima. The president of the office, Makoto Tanijiri, is a young but talented architect, and other members in Suppose Design Ofice also suceed in designing such modern architecture as housing and interior with their young spirit. What we strongly believe is only the architecture which exploits the full potential of "sites" by creating architectural forms on various conditions or situations can produce rich space.

Strong will and pliable ideas are definitely needed to exceed our present techniques and experiences and to develop ourselves.

We, Suppose Design Office, will explore the possibilities of sites and architecture through our activities.

Architects:	Turner + Associates Architects
Address:	Level 2, 410 Crown Street Surry Hills NSW 2010 Australia
Tel.:	+612 9690 2855
Fax:	+612 9690 2411
Email:	office@turnerassociates.com.au
Web:	www.turnerassociates.com.au

Turner + Associates Architects

We believe that architecture should be satisfying to use, visually engaging, cost effective to build and operate, sustainable in its use of natural resources and borne from innovative yet pragmatic responses to briefs, sites and typologies.

The team of 35 is driven by a desire for understanding the contemporary urban landscape and for facilitating its repair and reinvention through application of these guiding principles.

A collaborative process informs all of the projects. We see ourselves as part of a design team including our client and consultants. We actively seek collaborative input at the earliest point so that each project benefits from appropriate expertise in other fields.

Our projects currently include large-scale masterplans, mixed-use urban renewal projects, residential, commercial and industrial developments, both throughout Australia and internationally.

Architects:	Stadhouderskade 113
Address:	Postbus 75381 1070 AJ Amsterdam
Tel.:	+31 20 570 20 40
Fax:	+31 20 570 20 41
Email:	info@unstudio.com
Web:	www.unstudio.com

Architects:	wulf & partner
	Freie Architekten BDA
	Prof. Tobias Wulf
Address:	Charlottenstraße 29-31 70182 Stuttgart Germany
Tel.:	0711-248917-0
Fax:	0711-248917-10
Email:	info@wulf-partner.de
Web:	www.wulf-partner.de

UNStudio

Founded in 1988 by Ben van Berkel and Caroline Bos UN Studio is a Dutch architectural design studio specialising in architecture, urban development and infrastructural projects. As a network practice, UN Studio approaches projects with a non-hierarchical, complex, generative and integral design process, organized in a contemporary way, and using technologies that allow for maximum exchange.

Although based in Amsterdam, the office has worked internationally since its beginning and has produced a wide range of work from public buildings, infrastructure, offices, living and products to urban masterplans.

UN Studio directors Ben van Berkel and Caroline Bos together with partners Tobias Wallisser and Harm Wassink and associate Gerard Loozekoot form the management team of the office.

Pivotal UN Studio projects within these fields include; the new Mercedes-Benz Museum in Stuttgart (2001-2006), the Erasmus Bridge in Rotterdam (1990-1996), the Office complex La Defense in Almere (1999-2004), the Möbius House in Het Gooi (1993-1998) and Arnhem Central Station (1996-2008).

wulf & partner

The aim of our endeavour is good architecture.

Our understanding is that each project is uniquely complex and therefore requires a tailor-made solution. We achieve this through a multivalent design process, enveloping all aspects of site, environmental, financial and deadline demands. The general, working structure of each of our projects is clearly reflected in their built form. These forms are not governed by (con)temporary fashions, but rather perpetually update themselves, embracing the influences and demands of our times, yet steeped in an understanding of architectural history and theory. Most important for us is the effect which our buildings will have on their users, our designs are playful whilst remaining objective. Freedom, clarity and an understanding of human needs, are ideals which we strive for in our architecture and similarly in our working ethic, which leads to a vibrant atmosphere and team spirit in our offices. Motivating factors of our work may be dreams, illusions and a utopian vision, but these are well balanced with a need for realisation.

Architects:	Zaha Hadid Architects
Address:	Studios 9, 10 Bowling Green Lane
	London EC1R 0BQ United Kingdom
Tel.:	+44 0207 253 5147
Fax:	+44 0207 251 8322
Email:	mail@zaha-hadid.com
Web:	www.zaha-hadid.com

Zaha Hadid Architects

Zaha Hadid is an architect who consistently pushes the boundaries of architecture and urban design. Her work experiments with new spatial concepts intensifying existing urban landscapes in the pursuit of a visionary aesthetic that encompasses all fields of design, ranging from urban scale through to products, interiors and furniture. Best known for her seminal built works (Vitra Fire Station, Land Formation-One, Bergisel Ski-Jump, Strasbourg Tram Station, the Rosenthal Centre for Contemporary Art in Cincinnati, the BMW Central Building in Leipzig, the Hotel Puerta America (interior) in Madrid, the Ordrupgaard Museum Extension in Copenhagen, and the Phaeno Science Center in Wolfsburg, her central concerns involve a simultaneous engagement in practice, teaching and research.